Building Faith
Brick by Brick II

Building Faith
Brick by Brick II

An Imaginative Way to Explore the Parables
with God's People

Emily Slichter Given

CHURCH
PUBLISHING
INCORPORATED

Illustrations by Tom Lybeck.
Photos provided by the author.

Church Publishing Incorporated
19 East 34th Street
New York, NY 10016

Cover design by: Beth Oberholtzer
Typeset by: Beth Oberholtzer

Printed in the United States of America

Library of Congress Cataloging-in-Publication Data

Names: Given, Emily Slichter, author.
Title: Building faith brick by brick II : an imaginative way to explore the Parables with God's people / Emily Slichter Given.
Description: 2 [edition]. | New York : Church Publishing Incorporated, 2019.
Identifiers: LCCN 2018041902 (print) | LCCN 2018048827 (ebook) | ISBN 9781640650923 | ISBN 9781640650916 (pbk.)
Subjects: LCSH: Jesus Christ—Parables—Study and teaching. | LEGO toys—Miscellanea.
Classification: LCC BT377 (ebook) | LCC BT377 .G58 2019 (print) | DDC 268/.432—dc23

LC record available at https://lccn.loc.gov/2018041902

ISBN: 978-1-64065-091-6
eBook ISBN: 978-1-64065-092-3

"For generations, we have heard the adage that those who 'pray together, stay together.' But a tidal wave of compelling and catalytic research in the last decade on gaming, design thinking, and digital storytelling has proven that communities that stay together, play together. Congregations are finally realizing that God has given an imagination, as well as a mind, to every person. And that imagination must be named and nurtured so that both liturgy and life are an experience of 'the seen and the unseen.' Emily Given has written an essential text to help anyone who wants to engage divine truths through holy play for all generations. The word *lego* is, in fact, the Danish word for 'play well.' Read this book and let Emily Given show you how playing well can teach all ages to pray well too."

—Patricia M. Lyons,
Missioner for Evangelism and Community Engagement, Episcopal Diocese of Washington and author of *Teaching Faith with Harry Potter*

"Parables are for everyone, as are LEGOs®. Using LEGOs® to respond to Jesus' parables will profoundly deepen and expand the faith of students *and* leaders. All ages are blessed when they are involved in using LEGO® bricks to build and to explore the kingdom of God. Emily's versatile new book is like going back for a second helping of dessert—you want more of a wonderfully good thing!"

—Gail M. Jackins, M.Ed.,
Faith Formation Coordinator, St. Cuthbert Episcopal Church, Houston, Texas

"No one in the Episcopal Church messages as well about our faith and the meaning of it as Emily Given. Having devoted much of her career to the spiritual formation of children, she has learned to shape her words with great care and how to convey the gospel in the most inclusive, welcoming manner that I have ever encountered. I have been privileged to serve in ministry with her and listen to her make many insightful comments about the Sunday lectionary in our staff Bible studies, as well as to hear her preach. Anything that she says, does, or writes is a gift to the wider faith community. Emily Given makes the Bible come alive."

—Marek Zabriskie,
Rector of Christ Church, Greenwich, Connecticut and author of *The Bible Challenge*

"*Building Faith Brick by Brick II* is a wonderfully creative resource you can use to literally create an encounter with God! Emily Given's out-of-the-box approach to breaking open the Word not only is creative and easy to follow, but it has also revitalized our faith-formation sessions. Our annual tradition of 'Building the City of God' has become an event the entire parish looks forward to. Attendance during these sessions is better than at any other time of the year. The children enthusiastically dig deep into the scripture stories to glean a better understanding of the parable, key characters, geographic location, and physical terrain. Working as a team, they create a three-dimensional representation of the story and are able to articulate the passage. Our entire community then gathers to celebrate the creations. Not only are the children becoming intentional disciples by proclaiming the Word of God, they are also are learning how to work as a team to build their Bible story brick by brick."

—Vici Armsby,
Pastoral Associate for Faith Formation, The Catholic Community of Our Lady of Victory and Our Lady of the Snow Mission, Troy, New York

"Emily Given's 'Brick by Brick' method is perfect for presenting the parables of Jesus to children. While other curricula may opt to explain a parable and distill a 'moral of the story' for children, this approach allows children to make their own meaning, in their own time. The Building Questions help us (children and adults alike) to look at each parable from different angles, uncovering for ourselves the deep truth that lies inside for each of us. While preserving mystery and wonder, this curriculum helps children build their own religious language, with which to shape their thoughts and feelings about God and about their place in the big story of God's people. When this is our approach to Christian education—sharing our stories, nurturing the wondering process, and providing opportunities for child-directed creative response—we walk alongside our children in their journey of faith without getting in the way, and we allow the spirit to move where it will."

—Catherine Montgomery,
Director of Children's Formation and Family Ministries,
Christ Episcopal Church, Ponte Vedra Beach, Florida

"Poets use words. A chef uses food. Composers use music. Artists use paint. There are countless ways we tell the stories of our lives . . . of our faith. Emily Given is a creative genius in offering children and children-at-heart a way to enter into, while becoming a part of, the parables of Jesus using LEGO® bricks. *Building Faith Brick by Brick* is a visual and sensory experience—one that challenges and inspires the participant to think out of the box. It's also great fun! Ideal for churches and other religious institutions, both *Brick by Brick* books are also wonderful resources for experiencing faith in the home."

—Roger Hutchison,
Director of Christian Formation and Parish Life, Palmer Memorial
Episcopal Church, in Houston, Texas, and author of *Jesus: God Among Us*

"Imaginative, formative, and practical! *Building Faith Brick by Brick* works because it teaches the Bible story by story in an interactive way that children love and understand. The lessons are detailed and easy for teachers to prepare. The building questions make it very comfortable to engage children with the lesson, especially for new teachers. This user-friendly book checks all the boxes for children's formation. A Christian formation director's dream!"

—Lyn Merchant,
Director of Children and Youth Ministries,
Grace Episcopal Church, Anderson, South Carolina

For Helen W. White,
who invited me (and so many) to read
scripture "as if it were the first time."

And for Ginger and Sarah,
who continue this holy work.

◖ ◗

With gratitude
for the one who believes
"another world is not only possible,
she is on her way."

Table of Contents

---

* The following parables are found in the first volume of *Building Faith Brick by Brick: An Imaginative Way to Explore the Bible with Children* (2014): The Parable of the Good Samaritan; The Parable of the Lost Sheep; and The Parable of the Prodigal Son.

The Beginning

Most good ideas spring from a need—often an immediate need. *Building Faith Brick by Brick: An Imaginative Way to Explore the Bible with Children* grew out of an eleventh-hour realization that there was a hole in the midweek family programming planned one winter. Somehow, I had overlooked first grade. It was an innocent mistake since only two first-grade boys were coming on Wednesday evenings. They would be arriving in just a few short hours and I needed to be ready to welcome them.

St. Cuthbert's Episcopal Church, Houston, Texas

What I knew *(deeply)* was that one of the boys would engage in nothing unless it was related to Star Wars or LEGO® bricks. The question then became, "How do I use this to my advantage?" I knew next to nothing about Star Wars, so in a pinch I turned to a possible LEGO® connection.

With just an hour to spare, I pooled the entire LEGO® collection from the nursery school, picked a story that seems right *(Jacob Wrestling with God),* and headed to the classroom to prepare the space. I remember praying over that room *(small, without a lot of floor space)* and the volunteer leader *(surprisingly rigid).* It was one of those "Oh God, here we go" type of prayers then I offered it up for God to do something—anything.

The boys were thrilled.

The volunteer felt like a champion.

I was saved.

God was glorified. *(Amen!)*

The combination of God's grace and my creativity melded together into a new way of doing theological reflection. We were reaching into the stories of God while digging deep down into an enormous bin of LEGOs®.

A divine pairing indeed.

New Learnings

When the first *Building Faith Brick by Brick* book was compiled, it was in response to others seeing what was happening in Dallas, then wanting to know more about where to find the resource we were using. The truth of the matter was that we were making it up as we went along, relying on the Holy Spirit to do something meaningful with it.

Social media posts started popping up with vivid images of children with smiling faces who were holding precious treasures of our common story. My inbox was filling up with requests for information and inspiration of how others might start using this concept in their specific context. It was a joy to see this unfolding with beauty and enlivened spirit. Since then, many faith communities across the country and around the world have become "master builders" of their faith through the use of this simple medium—LEGO® bricks.

What did I learn in all of it since the first go around? Five simple things that should have been obvious from the beginning.

This is not just for children. The subtitle of the first book was "An Imaginative Way to Explore the Bible with Children." You may notice that has changed for this second volume. Once I started branching out with other age groups, another level of wonder and power was revealed. People of all ages and stages need to be called into playfulness and wonder.

Once a story is owned and created, it cannot be put away. This is meant literally and figuratively. The act of listening, responding, and then reflecting in 3D uncovered a connection with the story that many other forms of Bible study have not done. Imagining the story and then dreaming it into being is a deeply formative and personal experience. I often found myself unable to dissemble the creations because they had become holy: icons, shrines, or sanctuaries. In the midst of even the most chaotic rooms, the goodness of God was made known and the Holy Spirit blew into the space.

It's clear that the stories were being created in both the external and internal places of our spiritual selves.

Playful exploration of the Bible can heal us. When we create something, it becomes a part of us. Opening up the scriptures in this way can help us recapture the joy and wonder that we may have unlearned as we have grown through the seasons of our lives. Our children are witnessing at a younger and younger age the broken (and beautiful) world in which we live . . . and how they fit into all of it. Marriages end. People die. Ones we love disappoint us. Our bodies are not always what we hope them to be. Our emotional lives can be complicated and painful. God does not create these realities, but God is in the midst of them with each of us. Letting the stories of God's people into our hearts can be an immensely healing experience. The examples they set for us give us hope, give us direction, and call us deeper. The transformational power of God working in and through the figures in the Bible can show us our own belovedness more clearly.

The story is still being lived out in each of us. Allowing ourselves to discover God and the love that God has for us in every page of scripture can help restore our fractured worldview and sense of self. Hearing the movement of God over all of time can help us realize that we are part of God's enduring promise. Each of us is a star shown to Abraham and Sarah. Each of us was carried through the Red Sea. Each of us stood at the foot of the cross. Each of us felt the rush of the Holy Spirit in the closed room. Each of us was sent out to grow the church—the church that would become who we are today and the church we are working to birth into the future.

The act of reflection can be more important than actually creating something. One of the biggest learnings was to not rush the prayer, reflection, and check-in time. On more than one occasion, groups were so deeply engaged in reflecting on the story or sharing about their day that very little time was left to actually construct the story. I don't recommend this becoming the normal pattern, but I have found that being sensitive to the need to share our personal stories can take priority over recreating the stories. Scripture reminds us of who we are, and being in community around it can be a life-changing experience. People will lift up deeply personal things when surrounded by love and acceptance. Experiences like those can be a whole other sacred place. Nurture that. Strive for that. Make space for that to grow.

St. Michael and All Angels Episcopal Church, Dallas, Texas

Building Faith Brick by Brick Stories

Riley

There is always that story, that child, who shows us the face of God. For me that person is Riley. Riley struggled with making anything related to the story and had a one-track mind that only wanted to pray for dead dinosaurs. After five weeks of disconnect, something remarkable happened. We gathered as a group for prayer, storytelling, and reflection on the building questions. We looked at suggested images as we often did, but this time something was wholly and holy different. Riley worked and worked, digging deep into his bucket, clearly on a mission. When it came time to display and discuss his work with me, Riley proudly presented a tiny creation consisting of three LEGO® pieces. It looked like a tiny clam shell with a single LEGO® figure nestled inside. After five long weeks, Riley slowly spoke the wisdom of the ages, "This is Jonah. The fish wasn't angry. The fish was a helper. This is Jonah and the whale. He was waiting. Waiting for God. Sometimes you need to wait for God, Ms. Emily."

I was standing in the presence of a pint-sized prophet. The Word of God was revealed in just a few plastic pieces and the heart of a child. It can happen anywhere if we are willing to show up, be present to one another, and wait for God.

Jack

We never know what will bind us together in this life. There are times and moments of connection that happen each day without us realizing their significance. That is, until difficult times come. One of the children where I once served walked into the hospital one day with what his parents thought was a terrible case of growing pains. It turned out that Jack was beginning a five-month journey through an aggressive and rare form of cancer.

On my way to the hospital, I gathered the healing balm of Pringles, Skittles, and a new set of LEGOs® that, when put together, formed a prehistoric flying bug. I also brought the ridiculously long prayer shawl I had knitted more than six months prior. I never knew who I was knitting it for until the call came from Jack's family. I guess it had always been for him.

As I sat by the bedside, it was the language of LEGO® that created a moment of normalcy. Jack and I were talking about how to put the next piece into the Batman haunted LEGO® house; what we were really having was Holy Communion. It was a Eucharist of laughter and potato chips that said that God's love is with us— at all times and in all places.

Laura Lee

The church where I grew up (in suburban Philadelphia) opens its doors each month for a community dinner that is equally attended by church members and the homeless community of the town. Christ Episcopal Church, Pottstown has become known as a safe and loving place through its emphasis on looking beyond their own doors to respond to a changing downtown. They recognize the need to adapt to the culture and answer the call to be of service.

I was invited one evening to talk about *Building Faith Brick by Brick* and to provide an opportunity for all those gathered to build. Often when I lead groups of this nature, I invite people to share their favorite Bible story or the first story they remember being told. This night was no different. There were a number of different stories created—the Last Supper, Jesus on the cross, Noah and the ark, the burning bush, the Tower of Babel, and many others. The table conversation was lively, yet the person who caught my attention was a woman named Laura Lee. She dug down into the clear plastic bin of LEGOs® to unearth a boat and then went to work creating a scene on her blue building plate. Laura Lee was creating the calming of the sea. I watched as her hands moved over the plastic pieces. She was talking to herself and when I tried to engage her in what she was creating, I clearly spooked her, so I backed away. When I strained to hear what she was saying to herself, I realized it was a familiar psalm. Since I am not very good at memorizing Bible passages, I needed to search keywords online to find out which she was reciting to herself. It was a paraphrase of the first verse of Psalm 46: "God is my refuge and my strength. God is always there helping." She repeated those words over and over as she built her creation.

Laura Lee sparked something within me. I started to look at the other creations being made by the homeless friends in the room. They were all protection stories—Daniel and the lion's den, Jonah and the whale, the Passover, and the flight out of Egypt. My heart was stirred. It is rare that I have the awareness of the immediacy of needing protection because I have a home with heat, food, and clothing inside. My family is healthy. My circle of friends is ever-present. I wondered what my faith would be like if I were on the street with so much uncertainty. Would I cling to God for protection or rail against God for being forgotten? (Or something else altogether?) It was then that I realized I was asking the wrong question. This moment wasn't really for me to draw conclusions on how Laura Lee and I were similar or different. The work for me in the moment was to recognize that we are the *same*. We were both God's precious ones. The question became, "How can I be aware enough to see that God was always helping as Laura Lee had been whispering?"

"The Last Supper" Our Lady of Victory Catholic Church, Troy, New York

Saint Michael and All Angels Afterschool Friends

The power of suggestion can be strong. Once one person prays for a dead pet, then the rest follow suit with tales of all their pets who have gone on to glory. The need to identify with others (and sometimes outdo others) is compelling. Early on in the *Building Faith* adventure, there was a group of extroverted children who loved to share "highs and lows" from their week as part of the circle check-in time. One child in that group divulged that his parents fought every night and that he was afraid. Much to my surprise this set off a trail of deeply personal reflections by nearly the entire group. Children spoke of overhearing fights at night or being caught in the car while their parents engaged in heated conversations. They shared stories of feeling low on the priority list or about the pain of absent parents due to work schedules, addiction, or emotional disconnection.

My heart was broken open—and apart. These children were carrying the world on their shoulders and in their spirit. It was then that I realized there are very few places throughout the week where we provide safe, honest spaces to reflect on life. The busy and stressful pace many of us keep does not allow for it.

Sometimes one simply needs to set the plan aside and listen. It is a qualitative sense of listening with your heart and allowing a space to show up for one another. We didn't get much built in the way of LEGO® creations that day, but we did learn a ton about what the kingdom of God feels like and sounds like. It was in that space that we knew how to exercise prayerful listening and hold a holy space for one another. Do not shy away from the difficult questions or stories. We are all yearning to share them. God will show up. It will be holy. I know it.

St. John's Episcopal Church, Georgetown, Washington, D.C.

A Case for Wondering

We have become a culture that expects prodigies in the halls of elementary schools and professional athletes on the playing fields. Performance and achievement are in hyperdrive in the lives of many of our children. There isn't a lot of room for dabbling in a few different interests. An "A Team" expectation has taken the place of backyard fun and schoolyard free play.

It is possible to step back from those expectations—children and adults alike. It is time to allow ourselves to enter into a place of wonder. A place of joyful unknowing. It may be scary at first, but that fear can break free into peaceful and fruitful exploration if we make room in our hearts, minds, and schedules.

In Bible studies I often say, "I don't know how God really works. If we figured it out, that would make God too small." I truly believe that statement. We can grow in faith and love of God without figuring out the ins and outs of the gift of grace and miracle of living. We do not need to perfect life; we need to live it, show up, and enjoy.

How? Open our hands. Unclench our jaws. Step back from the intensity . . . and wonder. Just wonder. "I don't know" can be one of the most informative and freeing phrases we can utter in our life of faith. Let's help to nurture a generation of God's people who can simply be in the presence of God and wonder.

I have watched the most emotionally unavailable people open like flowers when they were invited into the process of wondering. I have witnessed the most active children become deeply focused and connected when encouraged to find their wondering places. There have been truly amazing self-discoveries and theological awakenings around the *Lego My Bible* circles. Some of my most treasured time has been being present for "God moments" with children who, in new and renewed ways, access the holy places of their lives. I have no doubt that God continues to show up in really significant ways. I trust this will happen for your group too.

The meat of this book is the Building Questions. They are a series of wondering questions that are meant to draw us into the stories so we can allow them to transform our lives and inform our living. I have sat at the feet of people like Jerome Berryman, David Canan, Paul Carling, Vicki Garvey, Jeff Ross, Robyn Szoke, Helen White, Lisa Kimball, and Dana Toedtman long enough to witness the power of wonder. I was blessed to be born into a family with Ginny and Charlie Slichter, people who allowed the world to be enormously large and lovingly small. What kind of place will you create so that those around you can flourish and explore?

Note: Several of the lessons repeat the same questions over and over. This is intentional. In each record of faith told in the Bible, we can't ask too many questions about why it matters and how we are a part of the story. Many themes are related, and therefore asking the questions over and over can create a natural connection and continuum between our faith stories. God speaks to us in an epic love story. The stories are for all people. I believe these questions can be pulled out and used in biblical exploration by all ages—with or without LEGOs®. They can help almost any group to break open scripture together. Use the questions in this book with your church's leadership board, women's groups, youth gatherings, worship settings, sermon writing preparation, and more. We can all make a place in our lives for wonder. The questions we have allow for a place where greater community can be found and a deeper level of trust can be built. It is in the questions that we come to know one another and God more fully.

Wonder.

Just wonder.

St. Thomas' Episcopal Church, Whitemarsh, Ft. Washington, Pennsylvania

Finding Your Own Words:
The Gift of Retelling the Story

I love to listen to stories just as much as I love to tell them. Our Holy Scripture has deep roots in a shared oral tradition. Reading directly from the Bible is completely fine. Riley's spiritual connection with the Jonah story was the result of a time I read directly from a children's Bible. We were given the written words for our devotion and use, and sometimes the nature of the story or the time you have make reading directly the best option.

If you want to make the story sharing more intimate, try telling the story in your own words. It is a wonderful gift to each other when we take written stories, learn them, and then retell them by heart (and *with* heart). This does not mean memorization. It also does not mean taking unnecessary or wacky creative license. It *does* mean placing your heart and words into the center of the circle so the group gathered can get a little closer to God through your sharing.

Tips for Enriching the Sharing of Each Story:

- ○ Spend time in study and reflection.
- ○ Read and reread in preparation. Scripture can speak to us differently each time we open it.
- ○ Keep in mind the age of the group and subject matter in order to tune the length and content accordingly.
- ○ Take into account the learning styles of the group and provide avenues for as many styles as possible.
- ○ Trust children to hear the whole story of God. Avoid the temptation to "water down" the uncomfortable parts of the Bible.
- ○ Talk to others about what they know or remember about the story from their childhood. If you take yourself back to the place of youthful discovery, you may find the scripture breaks open in a different way.
- ○ Read from both chapter/verse Bible translations and picture Bibles.
- ○ Write down a few key words or phrases to help you, if needed.
- ○ Be gentle with yourself. There are many ways to share the stories of God.

Don't get caught up in thinking there is only one right way. God is still speaking—through you.

Reading Scripture with God's People

Let's be honest. Children are often more open to the words and messages of scripture than adults. Children have yet to "unlearn" the wonder and joy of the stories. They have no need to pin down facts and poke holes in the imaginative process to protect themselves. Children can allow for the stories to just "be" what they are and take them as their own.

Adults, on the other hand, can get far too mixed up in the need to prove or disprove then believe or disbelieve until they have put the ways of God into a box big enough to love but small enough to figure out.

We can take cues from our children. Let God be God, without qualifiers.

Where do I see this the most? The writings attributed to Moses. Children's Bibles (too often) slice and dice these stories to make them less messy and certainly less violent or scandalous. My answer: trust children. If they are in solid and caring relationships with adults who want to learn and process the messages God is communicating, children will be just fine.

When it comes to the literal or figurative nature of scripture, there is a lot of room. Depending on when and how we were formed as Christians, we can find ourselves at a number of different points on a continuum. If we look at books like Genesis, it is easy to get caught up in the details. Was it really six days of work and one of rest? Were Adam and Eve actual people? Were all types of animals really in the ark? What about the dinosaurs? How could people really live to be that old? If God loved those people, why wasn't it easier?

The answers might be yes *and* no, yet the important part is "Why does it matter?" The important work for us is noticing what the whole arc of the story is speaking into our lives. God creates. God loves. God calls people to come closer again and again. God has inspired people of every generation to write down and share the stories of our common faith.

Here is the best part—all of us continue to be a part of God's story.

This is not a call to abandon biblical scholarship. Rather, it is a call to invite people into the process of digging deeper and learning what many voices have to say. To the best of our knowledge, there were several writers of the book we know as Genesis. This doesn't take away from the importance of Moses. It actually means that enough people thought his story was important enough to add their wisdom and knowledge about the history of the Hebrew people. People have agendas and certain slants. The Bible writers were really no different than us. The key to remember is that God uses us all, no matter our perspective.

The *Building Faith Brick by Brick* Method (Revised)

General Guidelines

Age Range
○ Most commonly used with children kindergarten through fifth grade.
○ Often used for intergenerational gatherings.
○ Suited for anyone over the age of four.

Group Size
○ Small groups can effectively range from three to twenty people.
○ Adult-to-child ratio should be at least one adult to eight children for small groups.
○ Intergenerational gatherings can be of any size.
○ For children under age five, a ratio of one adult to three children is suggested. (Be careful with the size of the building bricks.)

St. John's Episcopal Church, Georgetown, Washington, D.C.

Potential Settings
○ Sunday school curriculum (30 minutes or more)
○ alternative to boring lesson options found in other curricula (15 minutes or more)
○ afterschool program (1 hour or more)
○ weekday club (1 hour or more)
○ family or inter-generational event (1 hour or more)
○ youth group retro activity (20 minutes or more)
○ VBS curriculum or supplement (1 hour or more)
○ childcare room option (open ended)
○ home and family devotional (open ended)
○ adult learning communities (40 minutes or more)

Preparation

Story Selection
○ The best stories tend to include action, adventure, drama, wonder, mystery, or suspense.
○ Provide a mix of well-known and more obscure stories to provide intrigue as well as to build biblical literacy.
○ Explore only one story each session.
○ Remember to think about the context of the story.
○ Select an age-appropriate translation of the Bible—picture or chapter/verse.
○ Use the same Bible for the entire span of sessions. This helps to reinforce that all of the stories are found in scripture.

Preparing the Space and Setting the Tone

❍ Pray over the space.

❍ Clear the room to maximize floor space. LEGO®ing is best done on the floor or ample tabletop surfaces.

❍ Place a Christ candle in the room. (It can be a good quality battery-powered candle if you are concerned about fire or safety.)

❍ Create a place for prayer and check in—akin to "circle time."

❍ Place the Bible and samples of artwork in the circle where the leader will sit.

❍ Establish a display and discussion space. A dedicated table or counter works best.

❍ Set up a snack area. Eating "family style" promotes conversation.

❍ Prepare participant supplies. See page 25 for more details.

St. Thomas' Episcopal Church, Whitemarsh, Ft. Washington, Pennsylvania

General Lesson Structure

Welcome to the Group

❍ Welcome each person into the room by a volunteer or leader.

❍ Name tags are key. The use of names is so important. It is also a helpful tool for people to begin to learn the names of one another.

❍ Give a bowl or bucket, building mat, and a few minifigures to each participant.

❍ Invite each person to fill their bowl or bucket with LEGOs® and encourage them to create freely while others arrive.

❍ Give a two-minute notice before the focused group time begins.

Note: To avoid mix-ups with bowls, use a dry erase marker to label each bowl or bucket with names. After trying a number of different styles and shapes, the large, square popcorn buckets found at the dollar store seem to work the best.

Lay the Foundation

❍ Background information has been provided for both the leader and the group. Details include placement in the biblical narrative and intended audience.

Did You Know?

❍ Additional background information is included in this section to spark interest and to provide a wider base of knowledge and context before the story is shared. Some of the facts included may need to be tailored to the particular age group.

Pray

❍ Light the Christ candle and pocket the matches.
❍ Invite each person voluntarily into some form of prayer:
— Write or draw prayers on brightly colored paper rectangles to build a brick prayer wall session by session.
— Etch-a-Sketches®.
— White boards.
— Toss a LEGO® brick into a central bucket for each prayer offered during the circle gathering. These prayers can be guided or unprompted.
— Magnetic letters on metal sheeting or baking trays.
— Popcorn prayers: children pop up to offer a short prayer when so moved.
— Post-It® note prayers: colorful notes can be stuck to the wall to build an ongoing prayer corner.
— Tying ribbons onto a net.
— Lighting candles or switching on battery-powered votives for each prayer.
— Group texts for teens or adults.

Check In: Give the group an opportunity to tell something new about their lives since the last session. Possible prompts are "Tell me something from your day." or "Tell me something that I would never know unless you told me."

Share the Story

❍ Introduce the story:
— Where can it be found in the Bible?
— What type of writing?
— Who was the initial audience?
❍ Share the story by reading or retelling it.
❍ Show different images of the story to help spark imagination (art books, original pieces, or online image sites).

Respond to the Story
Building Questions

❍ Allow time for "building" questions, comments, and insights. A list of questions is provided for each lesson. This can often be the most sacred part of the gathering. Try not to rush through the reflections. The interior life of the group will often emerge in the most astounding ways. This is where the bulk of the theological reflection can be heard and witnessed.
❍ The list is intentionally longer than needed for one session so that the lessons can be repeated with the same group over time. This also allows for the leader to pick and choose which questions fit best within the context or age level.
❍ Questions appropriate for all lessons:
— I wonder what it would be like to hear Jesus tell stories?
— I wonder why Jesus told so many stories?
— I wonder who tells stories to you?
— I wonder what stories you have inside of you?
— I wonder what Jesus is saying to us now?
— I wonder if you see yourself in this story?
— I wonder what the story tells us about God?
— I wonder what this story tells us about life?
— I wonder if you have ever been told a story that you didn't understand?
— I wonder if you have ever witnessed the Kingdom of Heaven?

Suggested Blueprints

○ *Building Faith Brick by Brick* is intended to be an open-ended theological reflection space using LEGO® bricks. The need to specifically script a response should be avoided. However, if a person is having a difficult time focusing in on a response to the story, a few suggested idea starters have been included, called "Blueprints." The suggestions should only be introduced as needed. Reading them to the whole group could hinder the creative process, so keep them for "as needed" moments.

○ Allow the Blueprint suggestions to be simple words or concepts to spark ideas within the imagination of the individual.

○ Set the expectation that something from the story must be constructed before any other creations can be made.

○ Be available to answer questions, review the story, or help "stuck" participants.

Share Responses to the Story

○ As people complete their creations, provide a place for temporary display.

○ Listen to the stories the participants want to share about their work. This can be one-on-one, or as a whole group, or both ways.

○ Optional: Take a photo of each person with their creation or the creation alone.

Further Reflection across all Ages

The first volume of the book has had a life beyond its original intention. When it came to my attention that adult learning groups were using the building questions to assist their scripture studies, I decided to add an additional reflection section that offers a deeper place for personal reflection that may (or may not) be a different conversation than those in the reflections of younger believers.

Share a Snack *(optional, yet highly recommended)*

○ Begin or end with a story-related snack, if possible.

○ Pray over the food and group gathered. This prayer can be led by a person of any age. It can be a wonderful place to help everyone exercise the art of praying aloud in groups.

Continue the Story

○ Encourage each person to show their work to another person and share something from the story or creative process.

○ Allow families to explore the story at home by e-mailing, online photo sharing, texting, eblasts, or making a take-home sheet with the Bible verse.

○ If possible, keep creations on display during the week in a location seen by other parts of the faith community.

St. Cuthbert's Episcopal Church, Houston, Texas

Frequently Asked Questions

St. John's Episcopal Church, Georgetown, Washington, D.C.

How do I get enough LEGO® pieces?

To experience the full range of creativity, it is helpful to have an ample quantity of LEGO® pieces. Possible sources are:

○ Borrow a supply from an onsite children's program (preschool, daycare, or school).

○ Ask for hand-me-downs from families with children aging out of LEGOs.®

○ Visit tag sales, thrift shops, online auction sites, and online recycling or swapping sites.

○ Request donations of LEGO® bricks (or money to purchase them). If asking for donations, be specific about the size of LEGO® desired.

○ Watch for seasonal sales and store coupons.

Do females like *Building Faith Brick by Brick*?

While it is important to think past gender in binary terms, females of all ages do respond to the art of spiritual LEGO®ing. I have had women or girls in almost every group and they have always come back for more. Even if the group is entirely male, it is still very important to present female stories of the Bible.

How do I avoid the temptation for people to make unrelated creations?

Careful selection of the story helps to keep the focus on what is presented that day. Stories must have obvious characters and plots that are easy to follow. It is also helpful for volunteers to informally move through the room reminding the group of the need to create a response to the story *before* they can move on to other, unrelated creation. Gentle redirection can take the form of "Tell me how this creation is connected to the story?" or "What could you make that reminds you of the story we just heard?" It is also good to have a "no gun or nonbiblical weapon" policy.

What do we really need?

○ Lots of extra body parts and minifigures.

○ A bowl or bucket for each child.

○ A building mat for each child. This helps to stretch out the options for creating a whole story scene and not just a few small pieces. LEGO® offers at least two sizes.

○ Snacks. Powerful conversations seem to happen over food.

○ A Bible with a good, engaging translation.

St. Cuthbert's Episcopal Church, Houston, Texas

Who makes the best volunteer?

The truth is that we work with the resources we have at any given moment. Never fear, God can do amazing things through any one of us. If you have the gift of options, here are some qualities that are valuable:

○ Flexible and creative.
○ Open to noise and a fair amount of organized chaos.
○ Have a fairly good knowledge of scripture and are able to field questions (or be comfortable with "I don't know, what do you think?").
○ Physically able to get down on the floor (and get back up again!). If key volunteers have physical limitations, it is possible to move the creative process to tables.

What translations are recommended for study, reflection, and use with groups?

○ *Harper-Collins Study Bible: New Revised Standard Version Bible* (HarperCollins, 1993).
○ *Common English Bible* (Abingdon, 2010).
○ *The Amplified Bible* (Zondervan, 1985).
○ *New American Standard Bible* (American Bible Society, 1991).
○ *The Message* (NavPress, 2004).
○ *The Story: Teen Edition* (Zondervan, 2011).
○ *New International Version* (International Bible Society, 1984).
○ *The Spark Story Bible* (Augsburg Fortress, 2009).
○ *The Jesus Storybook Bible* (Zondervan, 2007).

Note: You may discover some biblically inaccurate "junk" out there. Be careful! If you are unsure of what Bible to use, ask a trusted person—lay or ordained.

Parables: Simple Stories for Not So Simple Ideas

More than half of Jesus's teachings were done in parable form. He understood that his blessedness, God's greatness, and how we are to live in response was far more than human hearts and brains could contain. Jesus recognized the importance of drawing people together in conversation and reflection so the message of God's glory and purpose could be revealed.

The word "parable" has Latin and Greek roots in the concept of laying things beside one another for comparison. It is the literary art form of sharing a story that has levels of meaning so that a fuller understanding of something more complex can emerge. Parables are full of imagery and often draw on the cultural references of the day. In the case of Jesus's parables, agrarian and domestic references helped to put the larger themes and messages into a context his audience could understand.

While there are parables throughout the whole of scripture, the best known are those shared by Jesus in the Synoptic Gospels. Matthew, Mark, and Luke are known as the Synoptic Gospels because of their similar sequencing and manner of recounting the events in the life of Jesus. This book focuses exclusively on the parables told by Jesus.

Why a whole book on the parables? They are rich in imagery and ripe for reflection by people of all ages. The parables engage the mind and emotions, no matter what place you find yourself. More than other parts of scripture, they can speak into our lives in very different ways based on what is happening personally or collectively. They are timeless. References to the parables have worked their way into popular culture—prodigal sons, lost sheep, pearls of great price—have taken on another level of meaning in our current age. This book is intended to help learn, relearn, and unlearn what we think about Jesus's moral and spiritual teachings. The intention is for scripture to be broken open in a way that allows us to see ourselves. The purpose is to know a bit more about what community should look like and what waits for us when we gather as people creating the kingdom of God here in our midst.

St. John's Episcopal Church, Georgetown, Washington, D.C.

Another reason to offer these stories in this fashion is to hold a space for unknowing. Matthew referred to the parables as "mysteries." The temptation is to quickly find one definitive meaning for each parable. It is true; some parables are rather direct and seem to have a single meaning. Be careful not to fall into that trap too soon. The gift we give to one another when gathered for scripture study is to surrender to the "what if" these holy passages have for us. Our modern viewpoints can limit our understanding. We no longer live in an agrarian society or live within the confines of traditional gender roles. Parts of the parables may feel outdated, sexist, classist, racist, or irrelevant. Trust me, they are not. As you engage the stories through our current realities, know that God's love and Jesus's message to us are eternal. The parables may not mean what we think. It is also true that they do not mean what we hope. The parables may touch on parts of our journey that are hard to discuss, yet all of them are for us.

Definitive meaning is overrated. Our need to figure things out hinders our sense of wonder and openness. I have spent a fair amount of time leading Bible studies of all shapes and sizes. All too often the question is uttered (sometimes in frustration), "But what does it *really* mean?" We need to become comfortable with "I don't know." It is a legitimate answer to all our faith wonderings.

This book is an open invitation to allow the medium of LEGO® bricks to help further your sense of discovery and wonder. Jesus used the parables to illuminate the way for people. He also used them as a way to teach a "master class" for his closest followers. Let Jesus's parables illuminate, instruct, convict, encourage, and support your journey home.

One may also find this book helpful by expanding their sense of what the stories may be calling us to consider in our lives now. Let us ponder that the master in these stories need not always be God. It is possible that the parables bear witness to other sources of power (just and unjust). For example, the parable of the tenants can be more than God's people violently and repeatedly denying the messengers sent into their world. This parable can also be seen as a reflection of our economic, political, or social climate. How have we not heeded the repeated calls to be better stewards of environment or honored the valuable voices of our diverse prophetic voices? Let the stories permeate your soul and allow them to inform your heart and actions.

Take them as your own.

Sharing Parables in an Interfaith World

There was a time in American culture when Christianity was the dominant religious influence. The teachings of Jesus filtered their way into education, legal dealings, literary references, and societal norms. Jesus was the example and the moral compass for many.

This is no longer true. A variety of faith traditions and secular viewpoints inform our blended sense of culture and community. To uphold the significance of the parables, it is important to recognize that many faith traditions have a segment of their sacred writings dedicated to the exploration of parabolic teaching. The Qur'an seeks to illustrate the natural world and the world to come by using the cycles of vegetation just like the Christian parables of the sower or the weeds among the plants. Hindu parables include references to social strata just as the parables of Jesus make reference to one's place at the banquet table or use the status of worldly wealth. The theme of observing the law can be found in the parables as well as Hebrew Scripture.

St. John's Episcopal Church, Georgetown, Washington, D.C.

This gives us a vast landscape to understand the importance of Jesus's words. His teachings are in concert with many others faiths. The foundational messages offered in the parables speak across culture and time. Jesus, Allah, Brahma, prophets from the Hebrew Scriptures, and many other sacred teachers are pointing us all to a similar place—we are called to live into a beloved community here on earth so that it will show others (and ourselves) the nature of God.

Fight against the need to have one story be truer or more important than another. The collection of our holy stories moves us into the realm of the divine. As Christians, it is Jesus who we primarily look to for our wisdom and guidance. Let us rest in the assurance that God is working in and through each faith tradition so that a beautiful and diverse understanding of our relationship with God can be made known.

The Parables of Cloth and Wineskins
Matthew 9:14–17; Mark 2:18–22; Luke 5:33–39

Welcome to the Group

Lay the Foundation

❍ *Where is the story found in the Bible?* **New Testament**
❍ *What is its place in the biblical narrative?* **Jesus's teachings**
❍ *Who was Jesus teaching?* **Levi, Pharisees, tax collectors, and unnamed others**

Find the full description of Lay the Foundation on page 22.

Did You Know?

✔ Jesus's cousin, John the Baptist, also had disciples (followers).

✔ This is one of the first times the foretelling of Jesus's death is introduced into his teachings.

✔ "Fasting" means to intentionally go without something for a period of time as a form of prayer and devotion. Commonly it is understood to be food, but it can be anything of a sacrificial nature that points one toward prayer and reflection.

✔ Wineskins were made from the skin of sheep or goats.

✔ Being a tax collector in the ancient world had a negative association since they were known for being dishonest and unfair in their assessment and collection of taxes.

✔ Matthew was a tax collector. He may or may not be the same person named Levi.

✔ Pharisees were a group of people who kept close to the tradition and laws of Judaism.

Remember . . .

❍ A parable is a simple story that seeks to explain a more complex idea.
❍ Jesus used common images of the time to make the stories understandable.
❍ The root word "parable" comes from the Greek concept "to compare or lay alongside of each other."

Pray

God of new beginnings, fill us with your goodness. Open our minds to experience the many new ways you call us closer and prepare our hearts to follow you. Amen.

Share the Story

Suggestions for storytelling are detailed on page 23.

Respond to the Story

Invite each member of the group to use bricks and minifigures to respond to the story. This can be done individually or in small groups. Suggestions for how to support this form of theological reflection can be found on pages 23–24.

Building Questions

- I wonder if you have ever tried to repair or reuse something?
- I wonder if you have ever fasted? From food? From things? From activities?
- I wonder if you have ever made a really big change in your life?
- I wonder if you have ever tried to mix things that shouldn't be mixed?
- I wonder if it is possible for old things and new things to blend together?
- I wonder if something can become whole again?
- I wonder what Jesus was trying to tell the Pharisees and tax collectors?

Questions appropriate for all lessons see page 23.

Suggested Blueprints *(if needed)*

- Levi's house
- wineskins
- cloth
- Pharisees
- tax collectors
- Galilean village
- Jesus
- God
- Holy Spirit

Share Responses to the Story

Encourage each group member to share the creations they have made in response to the story. More details about sharing can be found on page 24.

Further Reflection across All Ages

The message of Jesus is one of transformation. His coming changed everything. Maybe the wineskins and cloth call us to consider that the blending of old and new can rarely happen by putting a patch on an existing garment or seal on the seam of a drinking vessel. Craftspeople of all kinds understand that it is hard to mix materials and create a cohesive product. Levi, a tax collector, was called to follow Jesus right before the parables of the cloth and wineskins. I wonder, what it was like to know that his whole life was about to change and that little of the old would translate into the new ways of living? He could not patch or mend what he knew. What do we need to leave behind to follow Jesus in a deeper way? When have we noticed the "seams are pulling" on our lives because we are practicing the act of patching instead of replacing?

It is possible that we should think about this call to change in larger terms than just personal transformation. How might the systems we are part of (or benefit from) a true sense of transformation? How might we be called to be a voice for relational and systemic transformation? What might we be called to do to create something new in our homes, neighborhoods, country, and world?

Share a Snack

- Serve banquet foods true to the period (roasted meats, chickpeas, grape juice, grapes, figs, pita).
- A budget-friendly alternative to the banquet foods listed above includes fig bars, crackers, fruit, and sliced deli meats.

Continue the Story

One way to deepen the learning experience and create a link between the group and formation in the home is to have builders show their creations to others in the group. For additional study and conversation at home, consider different ways to share the scripture passages as well as some of the Building Questions. Possible methods of communication include group texts, social media posts, eblasts, online photo sharing, and printed take-home sheets.

The Parables of Salt and Light
Matthew 5:13–16; Mark 4:21–23; Luke 8:16, 11:33

The parable of salt is only found in the Gospel of Matthew.

Welcome to the Group

Lay the Foundation

- ○ *Where is the story found in the Bible?* **New Testament**
- ○ *What is its place in the biblical narrative?* **Jesus's teachings**
- ○ *Who was Jesus teaching?* **Disciples**

Find the full description of Lay the Foundation on page 22.

Did You Know?

✔ The Gospel of Matthew refers to this portion of scripture as the "Sermon on the Mount" while the Gospel of Luke calls it the "Sermon on the Plain." Scholars are uncertain if these two portions are the retelling of one single event or two different teaching moments.

✔ The location of the teaching is key. The fact that Jesus is going up a mountain to establish a place apart from the crowds echoes the story of Moses receiving the Ten Commandments in the Hebrew Scriptures (Exodus).

✔ Salt was used in ancient times as a flavoring as well as a preservative for food.

✔ Salt was so valuable that it was sometimes used as currency (money). It is even believed to be the root of the modern word "salary."

✔ Light is referenced throughout scripture as a symbol for creation, goodness, and the presence of God.

Remember . . .

- ○ A parable is a simple story that seeks to explain a more complex idea.
- ○ Jesus used common images of the time to make the stories understandable.
- ○ The root word "parable" comes from the Greek concept "to compare or lay alongside of each other."

Pray

Jesus, you have called us to be salt and light. Help us to create brightness and beauty in the world around us. Give us strength and courage to let our light shine in the darkness. Make us bold in our love and gentle in our mercy. Let justice be on our lips, in our hearts, and in our actions. Amen.

Share the Story

Suggestions for storytelling are detailed on page 23.

Respond to the Story

Invite each member of the group to use bricks and minifigures to respond to the story. This can be done individually or in small groups. Suggestions for how to support this form of theological reflection can be found on pages 23–24.

Building Questions

❍ I wonder what it was like to be a disciple?
❍ I wonder if you have witnessed the light of God somewhere?
❍ I wonder if you have seen the light of God in someone today?
❍ I wonder if you have been a light for someone else?
❍ I wonder what it feels like to lose saltiness?
❍ I wonder if you have ever felt like you lost your purpose?
❍ I wonder what you might do so that others can experience the love and power of God?

Questions appropriate for all lessons see page 23.

Suggested Blueprints *(if needed)*

❍ salt
❍ light
❍ disciples
❍ mountain setting
❍ God
❍ Jesus
❍ Holy Spirit

Share Responses to the Story

Encourage each group member to share the creations they have made in response to the story. More details about sharing can be found on page 24.

Further Reflection across All Ages

Our ability to stay open to the message of God is a true gift. We receive countless messages throughout the day that obscure our vision and distract us from our central tasks as followers of Jesus. Advertising and social media create a distorted sense of value, and far too often we use it as a measuring stick to wrongly judge our worth. What would it take to focus on being a light in the world? How would we live differently if we believed that our unique flavor of saltiness would bring a richness to our part of the kingdom? How might our hearing of God's message inform our actions? What might we need to put aside that casts a shadow over the beautiful ways we could illuminate the paths of justice, mercy, and grace?

Share a Snack

❍ salty food such as chips or pretzels
❍ fruit and veggies in "light" colors such as red and yellow peppers, white grapes, pineapple, watermelon

Continue the Story

One way to deepen the learning experience and create a link between the group and formation in the home is to have builders show their creations to others in the group. For additional study and conversation at home, consider different ways to share the scripture passages as well as some of the Building Questions. Possible methods of communication include group texts, social media posts, eblasts, online photo sharing, and printed take-home sheets.

The Parable of Two Foundations
Matthew 7:24–27; Luke 6:46–49

Welcome to the Group
Lay the Foundation

- ○ *Where is the story found in the Bible?* **New Testament**
- ○ *What is its place in the biblical narrative?* **Jesus's teachings**
- ○ *Who was Jesus teaching?* **Disciples**

Find the full description of Lay the Foundation on page 22.

Did You Know?

✔ The Gospel of Matthew refers to this portion of scripture as the "Sermon on the Mount" while the Gospel of Luke is called the "Sermon on the Plain." Scholars are uncertain if these two portions are the retelling of one single event or two different teaching moments.

✔ In the Gospel of Matthew, the water source is a storm while in the Gospel of Luke, it is a burst in a river.

✔ The Sea of Galilee is roughly sixty-four square miles.

✔ Another name of this body of water is "Kinneret," which means "violin" in Hebrew.

✔ The Sea of Galilee is also called the Lake of Gennesaret.

Remember . . .

- ○ A parable is a simple story that seeks to explain a more complex idea.
- ○ Jesus used common images of the time to make the stories understandable.
- ○ The root word "parable" comes from the Greek concept "to compare or lay alongside of each other."

Pray

Jesus, our true foundation, keep us grounded in your word and focused on your truth so that we can live in joy, peace, and hope all our days. When the storms of life surround us, remind us that you are our rock and safe place. Amen.

Share the Story

Suggestions for storytelling are detailed on page 23.

Respond to the Story

Invite each member of the group to use bricks and minifigures to respond to the story. This can be done individually or in small groups. Suggestions for how to support this form of theological reflection can be found on pages 23–24.

Building Questions

○ I wonder if you have ever been caught in a storm?

○ I wonder if you have ever felt like something important has washed away?

○ I wonder what it is like to be a builder?

○ I wonder if you have ever felt the safety of God's presence?

○ I wonder what it means to build on the rock?

○ I wonder what Jesus was trying to tell his disciples?

Questions appropriate for all lessons see page 23.

Suggested Blueprints *(if needed)*

○ house
○ rock
○ storms
○ river
○ sand
○ disciples
○ Sea of Galilee
○ God
○ Jesus
○ Holy Spirit

Share Responses to the Story

Encourage each group member to share the creations they have made in response to the story. More details about sharing can be found on page 24.

Further Reflection across All Ages

The amazing part of Jesus's teachings was the authority with which he spoke. It was done in a manner that surpassed traditional teachers of the time. The crowds knew there was something fundamentally different about Jesus and his message. He had come to show us the true foundation on which to build our entire existence. Where have you experienced the foundation of God's presence in your life? When have you felt as though your footing was on sinking sand? How do you decide where to build up your life? What are the floods or the storms you have experienced? How did you weather them? With whom did you weather them?

Share a Snack

○ yogurt or pudding topped with graham cracker "sand"
○ oyster cracker "rocks"
○ blue gelatin "water"
○ cookie building "blocks" with frosting "mortar"
○ cracker building "blocks" with nut butter "mortar"
○ rice cereal building "blocks"

Continue the Story

One way to deepen the learning experience and create a link between the group and formation in the home is to have builders show their creations to others in the group. For additional study and conversation at home, consider different ways to share the scripture passages as well as some of the Building Questions. Possible methods of communication include group texts, social media posts, eblasts, online photo sharing, and printed take-home sheets.

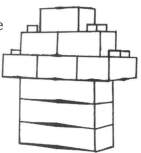

The Parable of the Generous Lender
Luke 7:36–50

Accounts of the unnamed woman can also be found in Matthew 26:6–13; Mark 14:3–9; John 12:1–8.

Welcome to the Group
Lay the Foundation

○ *Where is the story found in the Bible?* **New Testament**
○ *What is its place in the biblical narrative?* **Jesus's teachings**
○ *Who was Jesus teaching?* **Simon the Pharisee, the woman who anointed Jesus, and other unnamed dinner guests**

Find the full description of Lay the Foundation on page 22.

Did You Know?

✔ Meals during Jesus's time were often consumed at lower tables with reclining couches or pillows.

✔ A denarius (plural: denarii) was a silver coin used as a form of Roman currency (money).

✔ A "denarius" was approximately the amount of money a day laborer would earn for a full day's work.

✔ Perfume served numerous purposes during Jesus's time. It was used as deodorant, medicine, in worship, and for preparing bodies after death.

Remember . . .

○ A parable is a simple story that seeks to explain a more complex idea.
○ Jesus used common images of the time to make the stories understandable.
○ The root word "parable" comes from the Greek concept "to compare or lay alongside of each other."

Pray

Dear God, we want to always give our best to you. Help us to be unafraid to love and quick to forgive. Inspire us to make space to include all your people. Amen.

Share the Story

Suggestions for storytelling are detailed on page 23.

Respond to the Story

Invite each member of the group to use bricks and minifigures to respond to the story. This can be done individually or in small groups. Suggestions for how to support this form of theological reflection can be found on pages 23–24. You may also wish to use a sensory experience in your response. With the rise in the popularity of essential oils, many of the perfumes used during ancient times are able to be found in stores and online. The most common are sandalwood, cinnamon, frankincense, myrrh, and cypress. Others to look for are hyssop, cedarwood, and myrtle.

Building Questions

- ❍ I wonder what it would be like to be close to Jesus?
- ❍ I wonder if you have ever felt a deep sadness?
- ❍ I wonder if others have ever said bad things about you?
- ❍ I wonder if you have ever felt unloved?
- ❍ I wonder if you have ever asked for forgiveness?
- ❍ I wonder if anyone else has asked you for forgiveness?
- ❍ I wonder what precious gift you would give to Jesus?
- ❍ I wonder if you have ever asked God for healing?

Questions appropriate for all lessons see page 23.

Suggested Blueprints *(if needed)*

- ❍ Simon's house
- ❍ Simon
- ❍ the woman
- ❍ the dinner party
- ❍ Jesus
- ❍ God
- ❍ Holy Spirit
- ❍ kingdom of God

Share Responses to the Story

Encourage each group member to share the creations they have made in response to the story. More details about sharing can be found on page 24.

Further Reflection across All Ages

The point of Jesus's coming was to embody the love of God. When we allow ourselves to be raw and fully available to the healing presence of God, a fullness of life can be realized. We can be quick to discount the value of figures like the unnamed woman.

Let us be diligent in seeing the value in one another despite gender, class, sexual orientation, and racial biases. What if we sought the love and acceptance of God instead of others? What if we truly believed the only things which separate us from God are the things we place in the way ourselves? What if we gave our best to God without counting the cost? How would we be transformed if we saw ourselves in the place of others? What if we espoused wisdom for other faith traditions and believed there were no "others"?

Share a Snack

- ❍ Serve banquet foods true to the period (roasted meats, chickpeas, grape juice, grapes, figs, pita).
- ❍ A budget-friendly alternative to the banquet foods listed above include fig bars, crackers, fruit, and sliced deli meats.

Continue the Story

One way to deepen the learning experience and create a link between the group and formation in the home is to have builders show their creations to others in the group. For additional study and conversation at home, consider different ways to share the scripture passages as well as some of the Building Questions. Possible methods of communication includes group texts, social media posts, eblasts, online photo sharing, and printed take-home sheets.

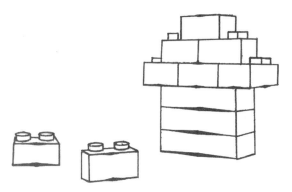

The Parable of the Seed Scatterer
Matthew 13:1–13; Mark 4:1–20; Luke 8:4–8

Welcome to the Group
Lay the Foundation

○ *Where is the story found in the Bible?* **New Testament**
○ *What is its place in the biblical narrative?* **Jesus's teachings**
○ *Who was Jesus teaching?* **A gathered crowd along the beach of the Sea of Galilee**

Find the full description of Lay the Foundation on page 22.

Did You Know?

✔ The method of throwing seeds with your hands is called "broadcasting."

✔ Generally, seeds break open and begin to grow within thirty-six hours of being planted.

Remember . . .

○ A parable is a simple story that seeks to explain a more complex idea.
○ Jesus used common images of the time to make the stories understandable.
○ The root word "parable" comes from both the Greek and Hebrew concept "to compare or lay alongside of each other."

Pray

God, our source of life and light, prepare our hearts to be like the good soil. Make the places in us ready to hear your word and do your work in the world. When we are thorny or feel dried up, give us your refreshing spirit. Keep us rooted in you, O God, so that we can live and grow in you all the days of our life. Tune our ears to hear your word so that we can live a rich and joyous life and spread your message to others. Amen.

Share the Story

Suggestions for storytelling are detailed on page 23. While the actual parable is only nine verses in length, it may be important to tag on the last eleven, which detail the interactions with Jesus and the disciples following Jesus's teaching of the crowds.

Respond to the Story

Invite each member of the group to use bricks and minifigures to respond to the story. This can be done individually or in small groups. Suggestions for how to support this form of theological reflection can be found on pages 23–24.

Building Questions

- ○ I wonder if you have ever planted seeds?
- ○ I wonder if you have ever tended something to help it grow?
- ○ I wonder if you have ever had a hard time listening?
- ○ I wonder what it feels like to be caught in a thorny patch?
- ○ I wonder if you have ever forgotten to take care of something?
- ○ I wonder if you have ever felt squeezed out?
- ○ I wonder what the sower was thinking?
- ○ I wonder why the sower didn't pay attention to where the seeds landed?

Questions appropriate for all lessons see page 23.

Suggested Blueprints *(if needed)*

- ○ seeds
- ○ sower
- ○ path
- ○ birds
- ○ rocky ground
- ○ thorny patch
- ○ good soil
- ○ field of grain
- ○ crowd
- ○ God
- ○ Jesus
- ○ Holy Spirit
- ○ kingdom of God

Share Responses to the Story

Encourage each group member to share the creations they have made in response to the story. More details about sharing can be found on page 24.

Further Reflection across All Ages

The temptation is to skim the surface of this parable and chalk it up to being a sketch of different types of people and their willingness to hear and heed God's word. While this is one of the only parables where a fairly specific explanation is immediately offered, resist the urge to leave it there. This parable has so much more to offer us. Is it possible that we possess all of these places within ourselves at any given time? We all have paths, thorny patches, and rich soil within us. The work for us as Christians is to consider the fruitfulness and health of our spiritual selves when we are responding from each of those places. Where do you notice your "dry" places? What is happening in your life when you notice that your soil is "rich"? How do you find ways to stay open to the word of God in the moment?

Share a Snack

- ○ crumpled cookie "soil" and gummy worms in tiny flower pots
- ○ cupcakes with crushed cookie "soil" toppings
- ○ bean sprouts, carrots, and hummus

Continue the Story

One way to deepen the learning experience and create a link between the group and formation in the home is to have builders show their creations to others in the group. For additional study and conversation at home, consider different ways to share the scripture passages as well as some of the Building Questions. Possible methods of communication include group texts, social media posts, eblasts, online photo sharing, and printed take-home sheets.

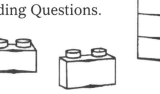
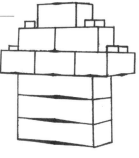

The Parable of Weeds and Plants
Matthew 13:24–30, 36–43

Welcome to the Group

Lay the Foundation

- *Where is the story found in the Bible?* **New Testament**
- *What is its place in the biblical narrative?* **Jesus's teachings**
- *Who was Jesus teaching?* **A gathered crowd along the beach of the Sea of Galilee**

Find the full description of Lay the Foundation on page 22.

Did You Know?

✔ The Hebrew word for wheat is "hittah" or "chittah."

Remember . . .

- A parable is a simple story that seeks to explain a more complex idea.
- Jesus used common images of the time to make the stories understandable.
- The root word "parable" comes from the Greek concept "to compare or lay alongside of each other."

Pray

Creator God, grow our roots deep and strong. Plant seeds of goodness in our souls and cultivate a desire to know you more. Amen.

Share the Story

Suggestions for storytelling are detailed on page 23.

Respond to the Story

Invite each member of the group to use bricks and minifigures to respond to the story. This can be done individually or in small groups. Suggestions for how to support this form of theological reflection can be found on pages 23–24.

Building Questions

- I wonder if you have ever planted seeds?
- I wonder if you have ever tended something to help it grow?
- I wonder what Jesus was trying to tell the crowd?
- I wonder how weeds find their way into the plantings?
- I wonder if weeds can ever be beautiful? Useful? Good?

Questions appropriate for all lessons see page 23.

Suggested Blueprints *(if needed)*

- ❍ field
- ❍ weeds
- ❍ wheat
- ❍ enemy
- ❍ master
- ❍ servants
- ❍ kingdom of heaven
- ❍ harvest
- ❍ barn
- ❍ crowd
- ❍ God
- ❍ Jesus
- ❍ Holy Spirit

Share Responses to the Story

Encourage each group member to share the creations they have made in response to the story. More details about sharing can be found on page 24.

Further Reflection across All Ages

As Christians, we are called to live in the world but not be of the world. What does this mean? Each day we move about and live our lives with a whole range of humanity. Goodness and wickedness are intermixed at every turn. How might we be called to fully live in the light of Christ in the midst of division, sickness, and differing values? How might we stay focused on our own path and grow our own roots instead of being quick to "uproot" ourselves or others?

The question may be how do we remain faithful to God while living within a certain context? When church isn't the church we hope for, it can be painful and disheartening. How do we remain in a place of love, positivity, and openness? How do we remain willing to engage?

This is another one of the parables that Jesus gives specific cues for his intended meaning. He outlines how this is a foretelling of the end of times and what will happen for those who follow the Son of Man or "the evil one." This is another chance to go deeper than that single, central meaning. Consider the "field" to be your life. Where have weeds been sown in your field? Who has done that sowing and why have we allowed for such precious real estate to be taken up with anything other than life-giving endeavors? What has our attention in a way that distracts us for God and our call to be a follower of Jesus?

Share a Snack

- ❍ bread with olive oil to dip
- ❍ crumbled chocolate cake "soil"
- ❍ brownie "field" with sunflower seeds and butterscotch chip "weeds"

Continue the Story

One way to deepen the learning experience and create a link between the group and formation in the home is to have builders show their creations to others in the group. For additional study and conversation at home, consider different ways to share the scripture passages as well as some of the Building Questions. Possible methods of communication include group texts, social media posts, eblasts, online photo sharing, and printed take-home sheets.

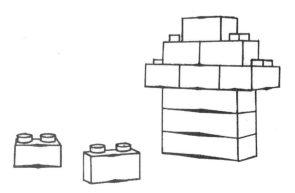

The Parable of the Mustard Seed
Matthew 13:31–32; Mark 4:30–32; Luke 13:18–19

Mark does not combine the parables of the mustard seed and the measure of yeast while Matthew and Luke do. Feel free to combine them into one session, if needed. A benefit to telling them together is to offer a space where both male and female images are present together.

Welcome to the Group

Lay the Foundation

- ○ *Where is the story found in the Bible?* **New Testament**
- ○ *What is its place in the biblical narrative?* **Jesus's teachings**
- ○ *Who was Jesus teaching?* **A gathered crowd along the beach of the Sea of Galilee**

Find the full description of Lay the Foundation on page 22.

Did You Know?

✔ The mustard seed referred to in this parable is not the variety of golden mustard you commonly find in the grocery store. The seed referred to by Jesus is the black mustard seed; barely visible to the eye, the seed is known to grow into maturity at nine feet.

Remember . . .

- ○ A parable is a simple story that seeks to explain a more complex idea.
- ○ Jesus used common images of the time to make the stories understandable.
- ○ The root word "parable" comes from the Greek concept "to compare or lay alongside of each other."

Pray

Heavenly God, our great sower, plant in our hearts the seeds of hope and forgiveness. Help them to grow and bear fruit so that all can know you and love you. Inspire in us the will to grow into the people whom you have made, loved, and called by name. Amen.

Share the Story

Suggestions for storytelling are detailed on page 23.

Respond to the Story

Invite each member of the group to use bricks and minifigures to respond to the story. This can be done individually or in small groups. Suggestions for how to support this form of theological reflection can be found on pages 23–24.

Building Questions

❍ I wonder if you have ever been surprised by something wonderful?

❍ I wonder how you might grow into something larger than you thought possible?

❍ I wonder how you might be helpful to others?

❍ I wonder what unique and beautiful things you can do with God's help?

❍ I wonder what about your life helps people know more about God's goodness?

❍ I wonder how you could tell others about the important stories of Jesus?

Questions appropriate for all lessons see page 23.

Suggested Blueprints *(if needed)*

❍ mustard seed
❍ shrub
❍ sower
❍ animals/birds
❍ crowd
❍ God
❍ Jesus
❍ Holy Spirit
❍ kingdom of God

Share Responses to the Story

Encourage each group member to share the creations they have made in response to the story. More details about sharing can be found on page 24.

Further Reflection across All Ages

The images found in the parables echo throughout scripture. The intention is to reinforce that Jesus was the fulfillment of many things. Jesus may have used the parables as a pep talk or playbook about how the disciples, as a tiny band of followers, were going to be crucial in the growing of the huge movement that would span space and time. If the disciples could truly understand, then they would be able to effectively and enthusiastically spread Jesus's message of God's love for all of God's people. Where might you serve as an active follower of Jesus? What might you need in the way of a pep talk? How might you seek to connect with God?

Share a Snack

❍ Construct tall pretzel "trees" together using pretzel sticks and marshmallow.

Note: Try to avoid reinforcing the incorrect image of using yellow mustard seeds and yellow mustard food products for this lesson.

Continue the Story

One way to deepen the learning experience and create a link between the group and formation in the home is to have builders show their creations to others in the group. For additional study and conversation at home, consider different ways to share the scripture passages as well as some of the Building Questions. Possible methods of communication include group texts, social media posts, eblasts, online photo sharing, and printed take-home sheets.

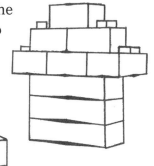

The Parable of the Measure of Yeast
Matthew 13:33; Luke 13:20–21

Mark does not combine the parables of the mustard seed and the measure of yeast while Matthew and Luke do. Feel free to combine them into one session, if needed. A benefit to telling them together is to offer a space where both male and female images are presented together.

Welcome to the Group
Lay the Foundation

- *Where is the story found in the Bible?* **New Testament**
- *What is its place in the biblical narrative?* **Jesus's teachings**
- *Who was Jesus teaching?* **A gathered crowd along the beach of the Sea of Galilee**

Find the full description of Lay the Foundation on page 22.

Did You Know?

✔ Three measures of leaven are enough to make fifty pounds of dough.

✔ Yeast uses sugar to create carbon dioxide, which make gas bubbles. Those bubbles make the dough rise.

Remember . . .

- A parable is a simple story that seeks to explain a more complex idea.
- Jesus used common images of the time to make the stories understandable.
- The root word "parable" comes from the Greek concept "to compare or lay alongside of each other."

Pray

Bubble up in us, Holy Spirit, so that we can be alive with your wonder and joy. Direct our ways and give us courage to do beautiful things in your name. Amen.

Share the Story

Suggestions for storytelling are detailed on page 23.

Respond to the Story

Invite each member of the group to use bricks and minifigures to respond to the story. This can be done individually or in small groups. Suggestions for how to support this form of theological reflection can be found on pages 23–24.

Building Questions

- ○ I wonder if you have ever made bread?
- ○ I wonder if you have ever felt something bubbling within you?
- ○ I wonder if you have watched something grow?
- ○ I wonder what Jesus was trying to tell the crowd?
- ○ I wonder what you can help to grow, with God's help?

Questions appropriate for all lessons see page 23.

Suggested Blueprints *(if needed)*

- ○ woman
- ○ leaven
- ○ dough
- ○ gathered crowd
- ○ God
- ○ Jesus
- ○ Holy Spirit
- ○ kingdom of God

Share Responses to the Story

Encourage each group member to share the creations they have made in response to the story. More details about sharing can be found on page 24.

Further Reflection across All Ages

It is often helpful to have more than one way to approach scripture. The parable of the measure of yeast lends itself to those who love cooking or have an interest in science. Baking bread is both an art and a science. The yeast, when folded into the dough, feeds on the sugar and gives off bubbles of carbon dioxide and alcohol. Depending on the length of your session, it may be possible to use quick-acting yeast as part of the lesson. If not, you can prepare another bowl of yeasted bread in advance then show the before and after.

Share a Snack

- ○ yeasted bread, sliced, with olive oil for dipping
- ○ Provide uncooked dough and allow individuals to sculpt or form their pieces. Place creations on wax paper and bake them while the story is being presented. To keep the creations identified, write the name of each individual on the wax paper next to their creation. The dough can also be sent home with baking instructions.

Continue the Story

One way to deepen the learning experience and create a link between the group and formation in the home is to have builders show their creations to others in the group. For additional study and conversation at home, consider different ways to share the scripture passages as well as some of the Building Questions. Possible methods of communication include group texts, social media posts, eblasts, online photo sharing, and printed take-home sheets.

Another idea to help promote faithful conversations at home is to give each person a packet of yeast and a simple recipe to make bread together. Invite people to light a candle and enjoy the bread together.

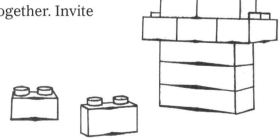

The Parables of the Hidden Treasure and Precious Pearl
Matthew 13:44–46

The Gospel of Matthew gathers the parables of the hidden treasure, the pearl, and the wide cast net together in one section. Depending on the number of sessions available to you, it is possible to split them up into three separate sessions or offer as one by combining lessons.

Welcome to the Group
Lay the Foundation

- ○ *Where is the story found in the Bible?* **New Testament**
- ○ *What is its place in the biblical narrative?* **Jesus's teachings**
- ○ *Who was Jesus teaching?* **A gathered crowd along the beach of the Sea of Galilee**

Find the full description of Lay the Foundation on page 22.

Did You Know?

✔ Pearls are still found to this day inside of oysters in the Persian Gulf.

✔ The Persian Gulf is mostly bordered by Iran and Saudi Arabia.

✔ The symbol of the pearl is considered to be precious because of their rarity and the complicated process to harvest them.

Remember . . .

- ○ A parable is a simple story that seeks to explain a more complex idea.
- ○ Jesus used common images of the time to make the stories understandable.
- ○ The root word "parable" comes from the Greek concept "to compare or lay alongside of each other."

Pray

Dear God, open our eyes to see what is truly precious. Direct our hearts to focus on those precious things and be willing to give up what gets in the way. Help us to see our own preciousness. Amen.

Share the Story

Suggestions for storytelling are detailed on page 23.

Respond to the Story

Invite each member of the group to use bricks and minifigures to respond to the story. This can be done individually or in small groups. Suggestions for how to support this form of theological reflection can be found on pages 23–24.

Building Questions

- ○ I wonder what is most precious, special, or treasured to you?
- ○ I wonder what is most precious, special, or treasured to God?
- ○ I wonder if you have found God's hidden treasure?
- ○ I wonder what you would give up to have God's treasure?
- ○ I wonder what it feels like to give everything up in order to focus on what is important?
- ○ I wonder what really matters to you?
- ○ I wonder what gets in your way of focusing on God?
- ○ I wonder if you can see your belovedness?

Questions appropriate for all lessons see page 23.

Suggested Blueprints *(if needed)*

- ○ woman
- ○ pearl
- ○ man
- ○ field
- ○ God
- ○ home
- ○ Jesus
- ○ Holy Spirit
- ○ kingdom of God

Share Responses to the Story

Encourage each group member to share the creations they have made in response to the story. More details about sharing can be found on page 24.

Further Reflection across All Ages

We live in a "value added" society. We give value to things that don't necessarily deserve it and then undervalue the truly beautiful aspects of our lives. How are you showing that Jesus is precious to you? What faith expressions are you exercising to make this known?

When our vision is clear and our values in check, it is commonly understood that nothing is more valuable than a life lived in God. In the complex "real world," what would it take to give up everything to become a follower? What would it look like if we embraced the value of simplification and saw joy and not denial? What if we knew the deep peace of focusing on what matters most? How would our schedules look different? How would the quality of our relationships change? How might we see others in a new light?

Share a Snack

- ○ popcorn "pearls"
- ○ crumbled chocolate cake "field" (Hide a small cross in a cake. Then, once found, talk about finding the treasure of Jesus. Invite each person to "dig" into their chocolate cake to avoid any choking hazards.)

Continue the Story

If you have access to real pearls, consider bringing them in for the group to see and touch. Allow each person to hold them in their hands to see their beauty. It is also helpful to show pictures of a pearl in its shell. Another way to deepen the learning experience and create a link between the group and formation in the home is to have builders show their creations to others in the group. For additional study and conversation at home, consider different ways to share the scripture passages as well as some of the Building Questions. Possible methods of communication include group texts, social media posts, eblasts, online photo sharing, and printed take-home sheets.

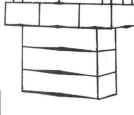

The Parable of the Wide Cast Net
Matthew 13:47–50

The Gospel of Matthew gathers the parables of the hidden treasure, the pearl, and the wide cast net together in one section. Depending on the number of sessions available to you, it is possible to split them up into three separate sessions or offer as one by combining lessons.

Welcome to the Group
Lay the Foundation

○ *Where is the story found in the Bible?* **New Testament**
○ *What is its place in the biblical narrative?* **Jesus's teachings**
○ *Who was Jesus teaching?* **A gathered crowd along the beach of the Sea of Galilee**

Find the full description of Lay the Foundation on page 22.

Did You Know?

✔ The nets used in the first century were generally round with weights fastened around the edges. They ranged widely in size. The nets were mostly thrown by hand or dropped off of boats. They required daily mending and washing to ensure their effectiveness and durability.

✔ The work of fishermen was extremely labor intensive and not a hobby or leisure activity.

✔ Some of Jesus's disciples were professional fishermen or had experience of living near the sea. A net was a familiar image and reference point. Jesus and the disciples knew the significance of keeping nets well-mended so that the best collection of fish would be possible with each cast. Jesus's call to be "fishers of people" was also hard work and demanded skill, attention, and care. This is important to note when drawing connections between fishing and evangelism. They are both very active pursuits that require active participation.

Remember . . .

○ A parable is a simple story that seeks to explain a more complex idea.
○ Jesus used common images of the time to make the stories understandable.
○ The root word "parable" comes from the Greek concept "to compare or lay alongside of each other."

Pray

God of enfolding love, help us to cast the net of love and acceptance as wide as our hearts can dream. Amen.

Share the Story

Suggestions for storytelling are detailed on page 23.

Respond to the Story

Invite each member of the group to use bricks and minifigures to respond to the story. This can be done individually or in small groups. Suggestions for how to support this form of theological reflection can be found on pages 23–24.

Building Questions

- ○ I wonder if you have ever used a net?
- ○ I wonder what it would be like to get caught in a net?
- ○ I wonder what it would be like to meet an angel?
- ○ I wonder what it's like to be wicked?
- ○ I wonder what it's like to be righteous?
- ○ I wonder if it's possible to be both wicked and righteous?
- ○ I wonder how God has called you?
- ○ I wonder how you might answer God's call?

Questions appropriate for all lessons see page 23.

Suggested Blueprints *(if needed)*

- ○ net
- ○ boat
- ○ fish (good and bad)
- ○ collection baskets
- ○ angels
- ○ furnace of fire
- ○ disciples
- ○ God
- ○ Jesus
- ○ Holy Spirit
- ○ kingdom of heaven

Share Responses to the Story

Encourage each group member to share the creations they have made in response to the story. More details about sharing can be found on page 24.

Further Reflection across All Ages

There can be deep discomfort in reading parables like the net. We can chafe from the rub of judgment or falsely assume our own righteousness. We may labor under the modern assumption that everyone should be "in" and that it is unkind to exclude. What does it mean that our loving and merciful God would send angels to "sort" through fish (people) and create death and "gnashing of teeth" (death and separation from God)? How do we balance the grounded and thoughtful understanding of the belovedness of all God's people with the call to live specifically as Christians? What does it mean to be sorted "in" versus cast "out"? Since this is one of the parables that Jesus immediately explains following its telling, we are left with the uncomfortable reality. In the end, it matters what we believe and how we live.

If we want to take it to an even more personal level, consider viewing this parable in a similar manner as the parable of the seed scatterer. It is possible that there are aspects of each of us that call for "angel sorting." The key is to be in constant reflection and evaluation of our lives so that there is far more righteousness than wickedness.

Share a Snack

- ○ gummy fish
- ○ fish crackers

Continue the Story

One way to deepen the learning experience and create a link between the group and formation in the home is to have builders show their creations to others in the group. For additional study and conversation at home, consider different ways to share the scripture passages as well as some of the Building Questions. Possible methods of communication include group texts, social media posts, eblasts, online photo sharing, and printed take-home sheets.

The Parable of the House Owner
Matthew 13:51–52

Welcome to the Group
Lay the Foundation

○ *Where is the story found in the Bible?* **New Testament**
○ *What is its place in the biblical narrative?* **Jesus's teachings**
○ *Who was Jesus teaching?* **A gathered crowd along the beach of the Sea of Galilee**

Find the full description of Lay the Foundation on page 22.

Did You Know?

✔ The role of a scribe is to copy writings down or act as a record keeper. They were the earliest "copy machines" before the invention of the printing press or other forms of mass-produced publications.

✔ The Gospel of Matthew referred to the disciples as scribes because their role was to learn from Jesus, keep record of his ministry, and then be prepared to go out to spread the message.

Remember . . .

○ A parable is a simple story that seeks to explain a more complex idea.
○ Jesus used common images of the time to make the stories understandable.
○ The root word "parable" comes from the Greek concept "to compare or lay alongside of each other."

Pray

Creator of the world, we give you glory and praise. Prepare our minds and hearts to hear your word and then grant us the courage to share your Good News with others. Help us to see your holy stories anew so that we can make them our own. Amen.

Share the Story

Suggestions for storytelling are detailed on page 23.

Respond to the Story

Invite each member of the group to use bricks and minifigures to respond to the story. This can be done individually or in small groups. Suggestions for how to support this form of theological reflection can be found on pages 23–24.

Building Questions

○ I wonder what you treasure?

○ I wonder what stories you might share to help others know more about Jesus?

○ I wonder if there is a difference between old and new treasures?

Questions appropriate for all lessons see page 23.

Suggested Blueprints *(if needed)*

○ home owner

○ treasure (old and new)

○ disciples

○ God

○ Jesus

○ Holy Spirit

○ kingdom of heaven

Share Responses to the Story

Encourage each group member to share the creations they have made in response to the story. More details about sharing can be found on page 24.

Further Reflection across All Ages

Scripture provides powerful examples of how God has moved throughout time and into the present moment. It is a treasured inheritance. Unlike the early followers of Jesus, we have the sacred writings of the Old and New Testaments to use for study and devotion. Imagine what it was like to form faith in real time as Jesus was walking the earth. Would it be easier to believe? Harder? Different? How might your faith be different if you didn't have more than two thousand years of history and sixty-six books from the Bible to shape you? What about scripture gets in the way of your faith? What do you feel you miss by not hearing the accounts of Jesus firsthand?

Share a Snack

○ A small, sweet treat encased in a small "treasure" box (a paper jewelry gift box or small wooden box, commonly found at crafts or dollar stores)

Continue the Story

One way to deepen the learning experience and create a link between the group and formation in the home is to have builders show their creations to others in the group. For additional study and conversation at home, consider different ways to share the scripture passages as well as some of the Building Questions. Possible methods of communication include group texts, social media posts, eblasts, online photo sharing, and printed take-home sheets.

The Parable of the Master and Servant
Luke 17:7–10

Welcome to the Group
Lay the Foundation

○ *Where is the story found in the Bible?* **New Testament**
○ *What is its place in the biblical narrative?* **Jesus's teachings**
○ *Who was Jesus teaching?* **Disciples**

Find the full description of Lay the Foundation on page 22.

Did You Know?

✔ The words "slave," "servant," and "worker" are used interchangeably in the Bible, depending upon the translation.

✔ The word "servant" also refers to those in special office or elected positions.

Remember . . .

○ A parable is a simple story that seeks to explain a more complex idea.
○ Jesus used common images of the time to make the stories understandable.
○ The root word "parable" comes from the Greek concept "to compare or lay alongside of each other."

Pray

God, thank you for giving us Jesus so that we can experience the deepest kind of love. Make our hearts ready to love with all that we have and all whom we are. Teach us to give without keeping score or expecting anything other than the joy of giving. Amen.

Share the Story

Suggestions for storytelling are detailed on page 23.

Respond to the Story

Invite each member of the group to use bricks and minifigures to respond to the story. This can be done individually or in small groups. Suggestions for how to support this form of theological reflection can be found on pages 23–24.

Building Questions

- ○ I wonder what it means to be a servant?
- ○ I wonder what it means to be a master?
- ○ I wonder if you have ever worked very hard?
- ○ I wonder if you have been in charge of something?
- ○ I wonder if you have ever done something to serve God?
- ○ I wonder if you have ever told others about Jesus? About God?

Questions appropriate for all lessons see page 23.

Suggested Blueprints *(if needed)*

- ○ servant
- ○ master
- ○ house
- ○ field
- ○ disciples
- ○ God
- ○ Jesus
- ○ Holy Spirit
- ○ kingdom of God

Share Responses to the Story

Encourage each group member to share the creations they have made in response to the story. More details about sharing can be found on page 24.

Further Reflection across All Ages

The word "worthless" is a rather loaded term. At first thought, one might think that the servant highlighted in this story is without value and is therefore expendable. Consider a different point of view. What if we saw our service to God as a natural part of our path? What if service to God was not a transactional affair? What would it look like to freely give our best to God without estimating the value of our gift? When you recall a time when you gave selflessly, what was that like? How did it change you? How did it change the receiver?

Share a Snack

- ○ Provide food that would have been served by the servant in this story (hummus, bread, grapes, figs, meat, herbs).
- ○ A budget-friendly alternative to the banquet foods listed above includes fig bars, crackers, fruit, and sliced deli meats.
- ○ Consider eating together on low tables or picnic style to help envision how a meal may have been served during this time.

Continue the Story

One way to deepen the learning experience and create a link between the group and formation in the home is to have builders show their creations to others in the group. For additional study and conversation at home, consider different ways to share the scripture passages as well as some of the Building Questions. Possible methods of communication include group texts, social media posts, eblasts, online photo sharing, and printed take-home sheets.

The Parable of Forgiveness
Matthew 18:21–35

Welcome to the Group
Lay the Foundation
- *Where is the story found in the Bible?* **New Testament**
- *What is its place in the biblical narrative?* **Jesus's teachings**
- *Who was Jesus teaching?* **Peter**

Find the full description of Lay the Foundation on page 22.

Did You Know?
✔ The number "seven" in the Bible often refers to wholeness or completion. Jesus's instruction to forgive seventy-seven times was meant to underline the importance of fully offering forgiveness to others without measure.

✔ A talent was a measurement of currency (money). One silver talent is roughly one hundred pounds. The modern value of a talent of gold would be over one million dollars. This measurement was used as an example of an amount that could never be repaid by a servant.

✔ Capernaum was the hometown of Peter.

✔ A denarius (a coin made of silver) is worth approximately four dollars in modern calculations. It was roughly the daily wage of a worker or the cost of ten donkeys at the time Jesus told this parable.

✔ The words "slave," "servant," and "worker" are used interchangeably in the Bible.

✔ The word "servant" also refers to those in special office or elected positions.

Remember . . .
- A parable is a simple story that seeks to explain a more complex idea.
- Jesus used common images of the time to make the stories understandable.
- The root word "parable" comes from the Greek concept "to compare or lay alongside of each other."

Pray
God of all people, open us to ask for forgiveness and ready us to offer forgiveness in return. Let us be people of mercy, peace, hope, and joy in a world that too often counts the cost. Help us to see that we belong to one another. Amen.

Share the Story
Suggestions for storytelling are detailed on page 23.

Respond to the Story

Invite each member of the group to use bricks and minifigures to respond to the story. This can be done individually or in small groups. Suggestions for how to support this form of theological reflection can be found on pages 23–24.

Building Questions

- ○ I wonder if you have ever asked for forgiveness?
- ○ I wonder what forgiveness feels like?
- ○ I wonder if you have ever forgiven anyone?
- ○ I wonder if there is a time when we shouldn't forgive?
- ○ I wonder if you have ever been in debt or felt like you owed someone?
- ○ I wonder if you have ever witnessed something that seemed unfair?
- ○ I wonder if you have ever given something without expecting anything in return?
- ○ I wonder what it feels like to really forgive from your heart?
- ○ I wonder if you have ever witnessed the kingdom of heaven?

Questions appropriate for all lessons see page 23.

Suggested Blueprints *(if needed)*

- ○ king
- ○ unforgiving servant
- ○ servant who wasn't forgiven
- ○ other servants
- ○ piles of money owed to someone
- ○ Peter
- ○ God
- ○ Jesus
- ○ Holy Spirit
- ○ kingdom of heaven

Share Responses to the Story

Encourage each group member to share the creations they have made in response to the story. More details about sharing can be found on page 24.

Further Reflection across All Ages

We live in a culture that places value on everything and assigned a cost equivalent to that value. Grades. Bank accounts. Outer appearances. The number of connections on social media. Far too many people are walking around constantly assessing their value based on any number of financial, relational, and spiritual markers. What would it be like to have a different measuring stick and source of value? Where would you look for that value? How would your relationship with yourself and others be different if your true worth was not based on external gauges but how God sees you?

Share a Snack

- ○ gold- or silver-wrapped chocolate coins that can be exchanged before eating
- ○ "silver dollar" (tiny) pancakes

Continue the Story

One way to deepen the learning experience and create a link between the group and formation in the home is to have builders show their creations to others in the group. For additional study and conversation at home, consider different ways to share the scripture passages as well as some of the Building Questions. Possible methods of communication include group texts, social media posts, eblasts, online photo sharing, and printed take-home sheets.

The Parable of True Friendship
Luke 11:5–10

Welcome to the Group
Lay the Foundation

❍ *Where is the story found in the Bible?* **New Testament**
❍ *What is its place in the biblical narrative?* **Jesus's teachings**
❍ *Who was Jesus teaching?* **An unnamed disciple**

Find the full description of Lay the Foundation on page 22.

Did You Know?

✔ Homes were commonly one room in the Middle East during the first century. Mats were rolled out in the evening to act as beds. Floors were compacted mud. Only people with wealth had more than one room.

✔ Families would settle in for sleeping earlier than modern families due to the lack of electrical power for lighting.

Remember . . .

❍ A parable is a simple story that seeks to explain a more complex idea.
❍ Jesus used common images of the time to make the stories understandable.
❍ The root word "parable" comes from the Greek concept "to compare or lay alongside of each other."

Pray

Jesus, may we turn to you in prayer, trusting that you will always care for us. Let us never grow tired of offering praise, sharing our concerns, and asking for your abundant blessings. Amen.

Share the Story

Suggestions for storytelling are detailed on page 23.

Respond to the Story

Invite each member of the group to use bricks and minifigures to respond to the story. This can be done individually or in small groups. Suggestions for how to support this form of theological reflection can be found on pages 23–24.

Building Questions

- ❍ I wonder if you talk to God?
- ❍ I wonder if you have heard or felt God talk to you?
- ❍ I wonder if you have needed help from a friend?
- ❍ I wonder if you have ever been a help to others?
- ❍ I wonder if you have ever asked God for help?
- ❍ I wonder how you might be a helper for God?

Questions appropriate for all lessons see page 23.

Suggested Blueprints *(if needed)*

- ❍ house
- ❍ asking friend
- ❍ sleeping friend and their family
- ❍ three loaves of bread
- ❍ the door
- ❍ fish
- ❍ snake
- ❍ God
- ❍ Jesus
- ❍ Holy Spirit
- ❍ kingdom of heaven

Share Responses to the Story

Encourage each group member to share the creations they have made in response to the story. More details about sharing can be found on page 24.

Further Reflection across All Ages

What does it feel like when you are searching more instead of having the sense of being found? What happens when you knock yet you do not feel a door opening? A life of faith is not just about waiting on God. It is a call to be active and listening in the present moment. What could you be doing to bring about the kingdom of God while you are knocking, seeking, and asking? How might you be persistent in prayer and engage in a life with God as you journey? Who needs a companion as they walk? Who is your companion?

Share a Snack

- ❍ three loaves of bread
- ❍ Construct (flat roof) houses with graham crackers and icing or marshmallow fluff.

Continue the Story

One way to deepen the learning experience and create a link between the group and formation in the home is to have builders show their creations to others in the group. For additional study and conversation at home, consider different ways to share the scripture passages as well as some of the Building Questions. Possible methods of communication include group texts, social media posts, eblasts, online photo sharing, and printed take-home sheets.

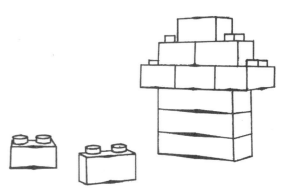

The Parable of the Guests and the Host
Luke 14:7–14

Welcome to the Group
Lay the Foundation

- ○ *Where is the story found in the Bible?* **New Testament**
- ○ *What is its place in the biblical narrative?* **Jesus's teachings**
- ○ *Who was Jesus teaching?* **Lawyers and Pharisees in the home of a Pharisee**

Find the full description of Lay the Foundation on page 22.

Did You Know?

- ✔ A wedding banquet is often used as an image for a heavenly feast.
- ✔ Wedding banquets lasted for several days during Jesus's time.
- ✔ Weddings occurred as young as the age of twelve in ancient traditions.
- ✔ Couples took part in a two-part process to be wed. The first was the betrothal (promise or engagement) and the second was the marriage. Both are legally binding contracts.
- ✔ Most marriages were arranged by parents during the time of Jesus.

Remember . . .

- ○ A parable is a simple story that seeks to explain a more complex idea.
- ○ Jesus used common images of the time to make the stories understandable.
- ○ The root word "parable" comes from the Greek concept "to compare or lay alongside of each other."

Pray

Dear God, thank you for setting a table and inviting us to come. May we always work to be sure all God's people have a rightful place at your table together. Let us seek to gather in ways that give us a small taste of heaven here and now. Amen.

Share the Story

Suggestions for storytelling are detailed on page 23.

Respond to the Story

Invite each member of the group to use bricks and minifigures to respond to the story. This can be done individually or in small groups. Suggestions for how to support this form of theological reflection can be found on pages 23–24.

Building Questions

- I wonder if you have ever been to a banquet?
- I wonder if you have ever sat in a place of honor?
- I wonder if you have ever been asked to move out of the way?
- I wonder if you have ever felt embarrassed?
- I wonder if you have ever felt like you didn't belong?
- I wonder if you have ever helped to host a dinner party?
- I wonder what it means to be a good host?
- I wonder who you would like to invite to your own banquet?
- I wonder who is missing from your table?
- I wonder who really needs to be asked to the banquet?

Questions appropriate for all lessons see page 23.

Suggested Blueprints *(if needed)*

- house
- table
- banquet foods
- seats
- party guests
- God
- Jesus
- Holy Spirit
- kingdom of heaven

Share Responses to the Story

Encourage each group member to share the creations they have made in response to the story. More details about sharing can be found on page 24.

Further Reflection across All Ages

We must always be asking, "Who is not at the table?" As followers of Christ, it is our responsibility to be mindful of making space for all of God's people. It is easy to focus on what is different about us or what separates us. What is harder, yet far more rewarding, is the ability to see those differences as beauty, giftedness, and what enriches us as a whole.

Who needs an invitation to come closer? Who else could be honored by the suggestion to "come up higher"? What if we believed that our belovedness is not based on status or position? What if we truly sought to see Christ in others? What if we allowed others to see the Christ in us?

Share a Snack

- Serve banquet foods (hummus, bread, grapes, figs, meat, herbs, grape juice, hard-boiled eggs).
- A budget-friendly alternative to the banquet foods listed above includes fig bars, crackers, fruit, and sliced deli meats.

Continue the Story

One way to deepen the learning experience and create a link between the group and formation in the home is to have builders show their creations to others in the group. For additional study and conversation at home, consider different ways to share the scripture passages as well as some of the Building Questions. Possible methods of communication include group texts, social media posts, eblasts, online photo sharing, and printed take-home sheets.

The Parable of the Feast
Luke 14:16–24

Welcome to the Group

Lay the Foundation

- ○ *Where is the story found in the Bible?* **New Testament**
- ○ *What is its place in the biblical narrative?* **Jesus's teachings**
- ○ *Who was Jesus teaching?* **Lawyers and Pharisees in the home of a Pharisee**

Find the full description of Lay the Foundation on page 22.

Did You Know?

✔ Banquet feasts lasted for several days during Jesus's time.

✔ A double invitation was communicated during this time. An initial invitation was issued in advance and then a second invitation was sent out at the time of the meal. It is similar to our custom of "save the date" notices.

Remember . . .

- ○ A parable is a simple story that seeks to explain a more complex idea.
- ○ Jesus used common images of the time to make the stories understandable.
- ○ The root word "parable" comes from the Greek concept "to compare or lay alongside of each other."

Pray

Inviting God, make us ready to accept your invitation. Help us open our doors and widen our circles so that everyone may know what it is to sit at the heavenly feast. Amen.

Share the Story

Suggestions for storytelling are detailed on page 23.

Respond to the Story

Invite each member of the group to use bricks and minifigures to respond to the story. This can be done individually or in small groups. Suggestions for how to support this form of theological reflection can be found on pages 23–24.

Building Questions

- ○ I wonder if you have ever felt called to the banquet of God?
- ○ I wonder who you would like to invite to your own banquet?
- ○ I wonder who is missing from your table?
- ○ I wonder who really needs to be asked to the banquet?
- ○ I wonder if someone has ever ignored your invitation?
- ○ I wonder if you have ever ignored the invitation of another?

Questions appropriate for all lessons see page 23.

Suggested Blueprints *(if needed)*

- ○ house
- ○ table
- ○ banquet foods
- ○ seats
- ○ those who did come
- ○ those who didn't come
- ○ party guests
- ○ God
- ○ Jesus
- ○ Holy Spirit
- ○ kingdom of heaven

Share Responses to the Story

Encourage each group member to share the creations they have made in response to the story. More details about sharing can be found on page 24.

Further Reflection across All Ages

I wonder if you have ever made excuses to avoid coming to the table, literally or figuratively? We tell ourselves stories of our self-importance or the need to be present elsewhere when all we really need to do is make ourselves available to God and one another. What have you used as excuses? You may not have a new plot of land, five yoke of oxen, or been newly married, but you may have had things happen that felt significant in the past or even the present. What are they and how important should they really be in your life?

Recall a time when you have been responsive and fully present to God and others. How did it feel? What made it different? What was the outcome? Life is all about choices. What will yours be?

Share a Snack

- ○ Serve banquet foods (hummus, bread, grapes, figs, meat, herbs, grape juice, hard-boiled eggs).
- ○ A budget-friendly alternative to the banquet foods listed above includes fig bars, crackers, fruit, and sliced deli meats.

Continue the Story

One way to deepen the learning experience and create a link between the group and formation in the home is to have builders show their creations to others in the group. For additional study and conversation at home, consider different ways to share the scripture passages as well as some of the Building Questions. Possible methods of communication include group texts, social media posts, eblasts, online photo sharing, and printed take-home sheets.

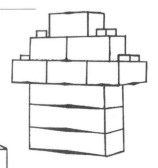

The Parable of the Cost of Following
Luke 14:25–33

Welcome to the Group
Lay the Foundation

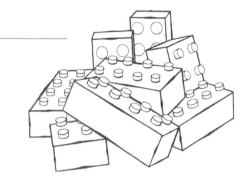

- ❍ *Where is the story found in the Bible?* **New Testament**
- ❍ *What is its place in the biblical narrative?* **Jesus's teachings**
- ❍ *Who was Jesus teaching?* **Large crowds**

Find the full description of Lay the Foundation on page 22.

Did You Know?

✔ The word "disciple" has its roots in the Greek and Latin words for "learner" or "student."

✔ The word "hate" in this context means to "detach" or "move away from."

Remember . . .

- ❍ A parable is a simple story that seeks to explain a more complex idea.
- ❍ Jesus used common images of the time to make the stories understandable.
- ❍ The root word "parable" comes from the Greek concept "to compare or lay alongside of each other."

Pray

Jesus, give us the strength and wisdom to follow you every day. Remind us that a life with you is better than anything else we can make for ourselves. Amen.

Share the Story

Suggestions for storytelling are detailed on page 23.

Respond to the Story

Invite each member of the group to use bricks and minifigures to respond to the story. This can be done individually or in small groups. Suggestions for how to support this form of theological reflection can be found on pages 23–24.

Building Questions

- ○ I wonder what it means to be a follower of Jesus?
- ○ I wonder what it means to you to "carry a cross"?
- ○ I wonder if you have done something important without a plan?
- ○ I wonder if you have ever made a really important decision?
- ○ I wonder what you would need to give up to follow Jesus?
- ○ I wonder what you would need to begin to follow Jesus?
- ○ I wonder if you have ever heard or felt Jesus call you?
- ○ I wonder what special gift you could offer God?

Questions appropriate for all lessons see page 23.

Suggested Blueprints *(if needed)*

- ○ large crowd listening to Jesus
- ○ disciples
- ○ family members
- ○ tower builders
- ○ king
- ○ soldiers
- ○ God
- ○ Jesus
- ○ Holy Spirit

Share Responses to the Story

Encourage each group member to share the creations they have made in response to the story. More details about sharing can be found on page 24.

Further Reflection across All Ages

What does it feel like when our guiding principles don't match up with the principles held by our friends and loved ones? Have you ever needed to end a relationship or move from that place of familiarity in order to follow your sense of call? What might God be calling you to do so that the kingdom of God can be made known to others? What are you willing to sacrifice? Who are you prepared to take along with you?

Share a Snack

- ○ cereal treat "building blocks"
- ○ mini pretzel rods to "map out" the path to follow Jesus. If laid end to end, they can create a fun road map. Paths can be windy, straight, or something in between. By laying a fresh table covering down, the whole table can become an intertwining map of paths to God.

Continue the Story

One way to deepen the learning experience and create a link between the group and formation in the home is to have builders show their creations to others in the group. For additional study and conversation at home, consider different ways to share the scripture passages as well as some of the Building Questions. Possible methods of communication include group texts, social media posts, eblasts, online photo sharing, and printed take-home sheets.

The Parable of the Lost Coin
Luke 15:8–10

The parables of the lost sheep, the lost coin, and the prodigal son (or forgiving parent) are very similar in nature. They can be told as a trio to help illustrate the importance of the joy in seeking and being found by God. The parable of the lost sheep and the prodigal son can be found in the first volume of Building Faith Brick by Brick.

Welcome to the Group

Lay the Foundation

- ○ *Where is the story found in the Bible?* **New Testament**
- ○ *What is its place in the biblical narrative?* **Jesus's teachings**
- ○ *Who is Jesus teaching?* **Pharisees, scribes, tax collectors, and sinners**

Find the full description of Lay the Foundation on page 22.

Did You Know?

✔ The coin from the parable is a "drachma." It is the equivalent of one day of a laborer's wages.

✔ In order to save ten days' wages, it would have taken many months.

✔ Gathering people together was a very common way to mark an important moment or to celebrate. This tradition carries on until this day.

Remember . . .

- ○ A parable is a simple story that seeks to explain a more complex idea.
- ○ Jesus used common images of the time to make the stories understandable.
- ○ The root word "parable" comes from the Greek concept "to compare or lay alongside of each other."

Pray

O God, who is always seeking after us, make us ready to be found. Prepare our hearts to rejoice in being your children and live in your ways. Let us be people who gather in celebration of the gifts you continue to give us and the way in which you show your love. Amen.

Share the Story

Suggestions for storytelling are detailed on page 23.

Respond to the Story

Invite each member of the group to use bricks and minifigures to respond to the story. This can be done individually or in small groups. Suggestions for how to support this form of theological reflection can be found on pages 23–24.

Building Questions

- ○ I wonder if you have ever lost something precious?
- ○ I wonder what it felt like to search for that precious thing?
- ○ I wonder what it felt like to find it?
- ○ I wonder if you have ever been lost? Or felt lost?
- ○ I wonder if you have ever been found?
- ○ I wonder how you would like to celebrate with God?

Questions appropriate for all lessons see page 23.

Suggested Blueprints *(if needed)*

- ○ house
- ○ woman
- ○ ten coins
- ○ friends
- ○ party or celebration
- ○ God
- ○ Jesus
- ○ Holy Spirit
- ○ kingdom of heaven

Share Responses to the Story

Encourage each group member to share the creations they have made in response to the story. More details about sharing can be found on page 24.

Further Reflection across All Ages

What if the important part of the process of finding the coin wasn't the coin at all? What if the true wealth was the joy the woman experiences in the act of finding the coin? How might you invite others to celebrate in the life you have found in God?

Share a Snack

- ○ gold- or silver-wrapped chocolate coins
- ○ "silver dollar" pancakes
- ○ miniwaffles
- ○ food fit for a celebration (Bible times or modern day)

Continue the Story

One way to deepen the learning experience and create a link between the group and formation in the home is to have builders show their creations to others in the group. For additional study and conversation at home, consider different ways to share the scripture passages as well as some of the Building Questions. Possible methods of communication include group texts, social media posts, eblasts, online photo sharing, and printed take-home sheets.

The Parable of Worldly Wealth
Luke 16:1–12

Welcome to the Group

Lay the Foundation

- *Where is the story found in the Bible?* **New Testament**
- *What is its place in the biblical narrative?* **Jesus's teachings**
- *Who was Jesus teaching?* **Disciples and Pharisees**

Find the full description of Lay the Foundation on page 22.

Did You Know?

✔ The word "steward" is used in many translations of the Bible. It is a synonym (similar word) for "manager" or "supervisor."

✔ Wheat was more valuable than olive oil in the first century.

Remember . . .

- A parable is a simple story that seeks to explain a more complex idea.
- Jesus used common images of the time to make the stories understandable.
- The root word "parable" comes from the Greek concept "to compare or lay alongside of each other."

Pray

Make us pure and honest, O God. Direct us to move through the world with goodness and love. Help us seek justice for all your people. Amen.

Share the Story

Suggestions for storytelling are detailed on page 23.

Respond to the Story

Invite each member of the group to use bricks and minifigures to respond to the story. This can be done individually or in small groups. Suggestions for how to support this form of theological reflection can be found on pages 23–24.

St. John's Episcopal Church, Georgetown, Washington, DC

Building Questions

- ❍ I wonder if you have ever been trusted with something important?
- ❍ I wonder if you have trusted others with something important?
- ❍ I wonder if you have ever known someone who has been dishonest?
- ❍ I wonder if anyone has called you dishonest?
- ❍ I wonder if you have ever asked for forgiveness?
- ❍ I wonder if you have ever had to set things right?
- ❍ I wonder if anyone has shown you mercy?
- ❍ I wonder if you have shown mercy to others?
- ❍ I wonder if you have done something so others would like you?
- ❍ I wonder what "true riches" are?
- ❍ I wonder how you get "true riches"?

Questions appropriate for all lessons see page 23.

Suggested Blueprints *(if needed)*

- ❍ manager
- ❍ master
- ❍ those who owed debts
- ❍ gallons of olive oil
- ❍ bushels of wheat
- ❍ God
- ❍ Jesus
- ❍ Holy Spirit
- ❍ kingdom of heaven

Share Responses to the Story

Encourage each group member to share the creations they have made in response to the story. More details about sharing can be found on page 24.

Further Reflection across All Ages

The desire to be liked is a strong one. When have you changed course in your life to save yourself or to win the good graces of others? Have you ever acted with questionable integrity? How did that feel and what consequences did it create for you and for others? What did you need to do to restore trust? How do you know when you are in right relationship with God and others? The invitation to be mindful is often quieter than the overruling call to get ahead. How might you make space to reflect on your actions and assess if they are in alignment with the call to love and care for others?

Share a Snack

- ❍ bread with small bowls of olive oil for dipping

Continue the Story

One way to deepen the learning experience and create a link between the group and formation in the home is to have builders show their creations to others in the group. For additional study and conversation at home, consider different ways to share the scripture passages as well as some of the Building Questions. Possible methods of communication include group texts, social media posts, eblasts, online photo sharing, and printed take-home sheets.

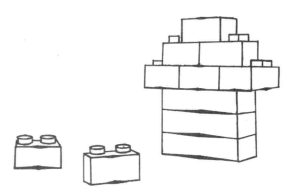

The Parable of Merciful Actions

Luke 16:19–31

Welcome to the Group

Lay the Foundation

- ❍ *Where is the story found in the Bible?* **New Testament**
- ❍ *What is its place in the biblical narrative?* **Jesus's teachings**
- ❍ *Who was Jesus teaching?* **Pharisees**

Find the full description of Lay the Foundation on page 22.

Did You Know?

✔ The color purple was only worn by wealthy people because it was costly to produce. The earliest source for purple pigment was the inner lining of a shellfish, slugs, and snails.

✔ The word "Hades" was considered the place of the dead in common Jewish understanding. It was thought to be a place of agony and unrest.

✔ Open wounds would have been considered "unclean" and a mark of sinfulness or wrongdoing in the time of Jesus.

Remember . . .

- ❍ A parable is a simple story that seeks to explain a more complex idea.
- ❍ Jesus used common images of the time to make the stories understandable.
- ❍ The root word "parable" comes from the Greek concept "to compare or lay alongside of each other."

Pray

Dear God, give us eyes to see the ones who others pass by. Give us hands to help and mouths to speak the truth so that we can share in the Good News of Jesus throughout the world. Amen.

Share the Story

Suggestions for storytelling are detailed on page 23.

Respond to the Story

Invite each member of the group to use bricks and minifigures to respond to the story. This can be done individually or in small groups. Suggestions for how to support this form of theological reflection can be found on pages 23–24.

Building Questions

- ❍ I wonder if the rich man ever thought about Lazarus?
- ❍ I wonder if you have ever been truly hungry?
- ❍ I wonder if you have felt like you were on the outside?
- ❍ I wonder when you have seen someone who needed help?
- ❍ I wonder if you have tried to communicate something important to others?

- I wonder if you have ever needed help?
- I wonder what it would be like to encounter an angel?
- I wonder how you imagine heaven?
- I wonder what it would be like to live in the presence of God all the time?
- I wonder how you imagine Hades?
- I wonder what it would be like to be separated from God?
- I wonder if you have ever been sorry for your behavior?
- I wonder if there is anything too big for God to forgive?

Questions appropriate for all lessons see page 23.

Suggested Blueprints *(if needed)*

- rich man
- Lazarus
- angels
- heaven
- Hades
- Abraham
- Moses
- house of the rich man's father
- the rich man's family
- God
- Jesus
- Holy Spirit

Share Responses to the Story

Encourage each group member to share the creations they have made in response to the story. More details about sharing can be found on page 24.

Further Reflection across All Ages

This parable is reminiscent of Charles Dickens's *A Christmas Carol*. The rich man is akin to Ebenezer Scrooge in that he has the opportunity to review the events of his life, see the error in his ways, and then wants to do something to make it right for others. Where the two stories diverge is the ability to go back. The rich man is of good intent to want to warn his brothers, but it is not possible. Actually, Abraham tells the rich man that it isn't necessary because the words of scripture are enough. What parts of scripture are the most compelling to you? Where do you see undeniable truth and wisdom that confirm your faith? If you are in a place of questioning, what words would foster your faith and bring you into a closer relationship with God?

Share a Snack

- grapes, thin pretzel sticks, and small cheese cubes (or marshmallows!) to use as construction material to build edible stick figures, the gate, or other aspects of the story

Continue the Story

One way to deepen the learning experience and create a link between the group and formation in the home is to have builders show their creations to others in the group. For additional study and conversation at home, consider different ways to share the scripture passages as well as some of the Building Questions. Possible methods of communication include group texts, social media posts, eblasts, online photo sharing, and printed take-home sheets.

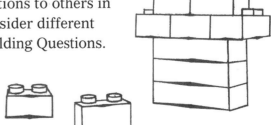

The Parable of the Day Laborers
Matthew 20:1–16

Welcome to the Group

Lay the Foundation

- ○ *Where is the story found in the Bible?* **New Testament**
- ○ *What is its place in the biblical narrative?* **Jesus's teachings**
- ○ *Who was Jesus teaching?* **Peter and the rest of the disciples**

Find the full description of Lay the Foundation on page 22.

Did You Know?

✔ A denarius was roughly the wage that would feed a working-class family for one day.

✔ Day laborers needed to be paid by sundown because it was considered the beginning of the next day.

Remember . . .

- ○ A parable is a simple story that seeks to explain a more complex idea.
- ○ Jesus used common images of the time to make the stories understandable.
- ○ The root word "parable" comes from the Greek concept "to compare or lay alongside of each other."

Pray

Dear God, keep us from jealousy, frustration, and the dangers of comparing ourselves with one another. Show us your bountiful goodness and endless mercy. Remind us that we are all your children and deserve your loving care. Amen.

Share the Story

Suggestions for storytelling are detailed on page 23.

Respond to the Story

Invite each member of the group to use bricks and minifigures to respond to the story. This can be done individually or in small groups. Suggestions for how to support this form of theological reflection can be found on pages 23–24.

Building Questions

○ I wonder if you have ever been surprised by the generosity of another person?

○ I wonder if you have shown generosity to others?

○ I wonder if you have ever worked hard?

○ I wonder if you have ever felt like something unfair happened to you?

○ I wonder if you have ever held a grudge?

○ I wonder if you have been to a vineyard?

○ I wonder what it means that "the first shall be last and the last shall be first"?

Questions appropriate for all lessons see page 23.

Suggested Blueprints *(if needed)*

○ landowners
○ workers
○ vineyard
○ God
○ Jesus
○ Holy Spirit
○ kingdom of heaven

Share Responses to the Story

Encourage each group member to share the creations they have made in response to the story. More details about sharing can be found on page 24.

Further Reflection across All Ages

It is ingrained in some people from an early age that "life is not fair." Life offers varied experiences that are not always the direct result of our actions or what is just. Think of the childhood chant "you get what you get and you don't get upset." What if the call to encounter in this parable is not the inequality of pay but instead the lavish sense of grace exhibited by the land owner? The kingdom of heaven does not have an economy that we can fully understand. Grace without measure and kindness without expectation in return can be foreign in the transactional world in which we live. When have you noticed jealousy creep into your heart? Has envy taken over when love would have better served you? How might you follow the example of the landowner by offering extravagant kindness and generosity? How might you work to make justice and goodness possible for all?

Share a Snack

○ grapes
○ raisins
○ grape juice

Continue the Story

One way to deepen the learning experience and create a link between the group and formation in the home is to have builders show their creations to others in the group. For additional study and conversation at home, consider different ways to share the scripture passages as well as some of the Building Questions. Possible methods of communication include group texts, social media posts, eblasts, online photo sharing, and printed take-home sheets.

The Parable of the Persistent Woman
Luke 18:2–8

Welcome to the Group
Lay the Foundation

- ○ *Where is the story found in the Bible?* **New Testament**
- ○ *What is its place in the biblical narrative?* **Jesus's teachings**
- ○ *Who was Jesus teaching?* **Disciples**

Find the full description of Lay the Foundation on page 22.

Did You Know?

✔ Widows were in a very vulnerable position because of their inability to own property, hold most forms of employment, or vote in the matters of the town.

✔ The original translation of "to wear him down" is very similar to the actions used by a boxer when worn out from fighting in the ring.

Remember . . .

- ○ A parable is a simple story that seeks to explain a more complex idea.
- ○ Jesus used common images of the time to make the stories understandable.
- ○ The root word "parable" comes from the Greek concept "to compare or lay alongside of each other."

Pray

Dear God, you are the one who hears the prayers we say with our voices as well as the ones whispered within our hearts. May we never grow tired of trusting in you and seeking your face. Amen.

Share the Story

Suggestions for storytelling are detailed on page 23.

Respond to the Story

Invite each member of the group to use bricks and minifigures to respond to the story. This can be done individually or in small groups. Suggestions for how to support this form of theological reflection can be found on pages 23–24.

Building Questions

- ❍ I wonder if you have ever felt like someone has wronged you?
- ❍ I wonder if you have ever needed to ask for help time and time again?
- ❍ I wonder if you have ever felt forgotten?
- ❍ I wonder what it is like to be a judge?
- ❍ I wonder if you have ever felt worn down?
- ❍ I wonder if you have ever done something to stop someone from bothering you?
- ❍ I wonder if God ever feels bothered?
- ❍ I wonder how life would be different if you didn't care about God or other people?
- ❍ I wonder what justice looks like?

Questions appropriate for all lessons see page 23.

Suggested Blueprints *(if needed)*

- ❍ persistent woman
- ❍ person who wronged the woman
- ❍ judge
- ❍ God
- ❍ Jesus
- ❍ Holy Spirit

Share Responses to the Story

Encourage each group member to share the creations they have made in response to the story. More details about sharing can be found on page 24.

Further Reflection across All Ages

Most of the parables point us to a greater truth about God or God's people. This parable may be a model of what we should be like in our relationship to God. Even though the odds weren't in the widow's favor, she continually came back to the judge over and over until she was given justice. This parable is a study in contrasts. We are called to persistence, not because of God's harsh and uncaring nature, but because of God's continual mercy and goodness. God wants us to be persistent in prayer and earnest in our belief. What is filling your time? How might you make space to be closer to God in prayer? What might your heart be asking for? Where do you need justice? Where are you actively seeking justice for others?

Share a Snack

- ❍ Since this parable is focused on prayer, consider making (or buying) pretzels and sharing the well-known story of how pretzels are another image for arms folded in prayer.

Continue the Story

One way to deepen the learning experience and create a link between the group and formation in the home is to have builders show their creations to others in the group. For additional study and conversation at home, consider different ways to share the scripture passages as well as some of the Building Questions. Possible methods of communication include group texts, social media posts, eblasts, online photo sharing, and printed take-home sheets.

The Parable of Humbleness
Luke 18:9–14

Welcome to the Group

Lay the Foundation

❍ *Where is the story found in the Bible?* **New Testament**
❍ *What is its place in the biblical narrative?* **Jesus's teachings**
❍ *Who was Jesus teaching?* **Disciples**

Find the full description of Lay the Foundation on page 22.

Did You Know?

✔ Pharisees were part of a Jewish group who lived a simple lifestyle and upheld more traditional views of the law.

✔ Tax collectors, also known as publicans, are often portrayed in a negative manner in the Bible. This is due to the concept that they were closely aligned with the Roman government and amassing their own fortune in unethical ways.

✔ Fasting is the act of giving something up for a period of time. Often people will give up something that gets in the way of their spiritual life in order to focus more closely on God for a specific time period.

✔ Fasting was only required once each year in the Jewish tradition on the Day of Atonement (also known as Yom Kippur). On this holiday, elaborate rituals are offered for forgiveness of sins. This tradition dates back to Aaron and can be found in the book of Leviticus.

Remember . . .

❍ A parable is a simple story that seeks to explain a more complex idea.
❍ Jesus used common images of the time to make the stories understandable.
❍ The root word "parable" comes from the Greek concept "to compare or lay alongside of each other."

Pray

Loving God, keep us focused on the right things. Teach us how to love you and all you have created. Remind us that showing off and bragging are not the ways to joy and peace. Amen.

Share the Story

Suggestions for storytelling are detailed on page 23.

Respond to the Story

Invite each member of the group to use bricks and minifigures to respond to the story. This can be done individually or in small groups. Suggestions for how to support this form of theological reflection can be found on pages 23–24.

Building Questions

○ I wonder if you have ever prayed?

○ I wonder how you pray to God?

○ I wonder if God has ever spoken to you?

○ I wonder if you have ever acted like you are better than other people?

○ I wonder if you have met someone who acts like they are better than you?

○ I wonder if it is possible to be right and wrong at the same time?

○ I wonder what forgiveness feels like?

○ I wonder what forgiveness looks like?

Questions appropriate for all lessons see page 23.

Suggested Blueprints *(if needed)*

○ tax collector

○ Pharisee

○ temple

○ the people the Pharisee thought were sinners

○ God

○ Jesus

○ Holy Spirit

Share Responses to the Story

Encourage each group member to share the creations they have made in response to the story. More details about sharing can be found on page 24.

Further Reflection across All Ages

Have you ever met a person whose words and actions don't match up? It is especially disheartening when someone who does all the "right" things does them for the "wrong reasons." If we are not careful, our worship of God can turn into idolatry instead of devotion. The Pharisee was following the letter of the law (and more), but his focus was on himself. In contrast, the tax collector recognized his wrongdoing and approached God with a humble heart.

While there are many messages in this parable, what might we consider about how we approach God in prayer? Have you ever come to God with more requests than prayers of gratitude? Have you engaged in worship more because you wanted to be seen doing the faithful thing instead of using it as a way to connect with God? It is good and right to be grateful for how we have been wonderfully made by God. Let us heed the caution of the danger of being overly proud and self-righteous. How might you stay prayerfully focused on walking the faithful and outward-looking path?

Share a Snack

○ Since this parable is focused on prayer, consider making (or buying) pretzels and sharing the well-known story of how pretzels are another image for arms folded in prayer.

Continue the Story

One way to deepen the learning experience and create a link between the group and formation in the home is to have builders show their creations to others in the group. For additional study and conversation at home, consider different ways to share the scripture passages as well as some of the Building Questions. Possible methods of communication include group texts, social media posts, eblasts, online photo sharing, and printed take-home sheets.

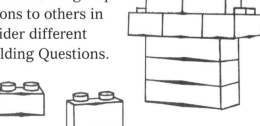

The Parables of Faithfulness
Matthew 25:14–30; Luke 19:12–27

Welcome to the Group
Lay the Foundation

- *Where is the story found in the Bible?* **New Testament**
- *What is its place in the biblical narrative?* **Jesus's teachings**
- *Who was Jesus teaching?* **Zacchaeus and his guests in Jericho (Luke); Jerusalem (Matthew)**

Find the full description of Lay the Foundation on page 22.

Did You Know?

✔ A pound was worth one hundred days' wages at the time of Jesus's telling of the story.

✔ The modern equivalent of a gold talent is 1.25 million dollars and 16,000 dollars for a silver one.

✔ Jericho was a main stop along a trade route.

✔ Taxation was an important part of the economic system of the Romans.

Remember . . .

- A parable is a simple story that seeks to explain a more complex idea.
- Jesus used common images of the time to make the stories understandable.
- The root word "parable" comes from the Greek concept "to compare or lay alongside of each other."

Pray

Creator God, inspire courage within us so that we can be bold in our love and constant in our care for others. May we be people who spread your word and spread goodness to others. Make us ready for your return. Amen.

Share the Story

Suggestions for storytelling are detailed on page 23.

Respond to the Story

Invite each member of the group to use bricks and minifigures to respond to the story. This can be done individually or in small groups. Suggestions for how to support this form of theological reflection can be found on pages 23–24.

Building Questions

○ I wonder if you have been trusted with something precious?

○ I wonder if you have worked hard to build or grow something?

○ I wonder what you might do to help grow God's love?

○ I wonder who shared God's love with you for the first time?

○ I wonder what God might be calling you to do with your life?

○ I wonder if you have held onto something and found it hard to share?

○ I wonder if you have ever felt afraid of someone?

○ I wonder if you have ever wanted to hide something?

○ I wonder what it feels like to "enter into the joy of your master"?

○ I wonder what the "outer darkness" is like?

○ I wonder if anything can really separate us from God?

Questions appropriate for all lessons see page 23.

Suggested Blueprints *(if needed)*

○ master
○ slaves
○ talents (Matthew) / pounds (Luke)
○ vineyard
○ field
○ Zacchaeus
○ God
○ Jesus
○ Holy Spirit
○ kingdom of heaven

Share Responses to the Story

Encourage each group member to share the creations they have made in response to the story. More details about sharing can be found on page 24.

Further Reflection across All Ages

God has entrusted us with so many remarkable resources. What does it feel like to be responsible for sharing the message of God's goodness? What parts of your heart and mind are eager to spread the message of the kingdom of God? What parts of you are more inclined to "bury" that message in the ground? How might you be able to offer a special window into your understanding of God's mercy and abundance?

Share a Snack

○ gold- or silver-wrapped chocolate coins
○ "silver dollar" pancakes

Continue the Story

One way to deepen the learning experience and create a link between the group and formation in the home is to have builders show their creations to others in the group. For additional study and conversation at home, consider different ways to share the scripture passages as well as some of the Building Questions. Possible methods of communication include group texts, social media posts, eblasts, online photo sharing, and printed take-home sheets.

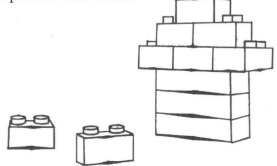

The Parable of the Two Sons
Matthew 21:28–32

It is possible to group the parables of the two sons, the tenants, and the host and guests together since they appear grouped in scripture.

Welcome to the Group
Lay the Foundation

○ *Where is the story found in the Bible?* **New Testament**
○ *What is its place in the biblical narrative?* **Jesus's teachings**
○ *Who was Jesus teaching?* **Chief Priests and Pharisees in Jerusalem**

Find the full description of Lay the Foundation on page 22.

Did You Know?

✔ The "John" mentioned in this passage is John the Baptist, cousin of Jesus.

✔ The first signs of settlement in Jerusalem date back to 4500 BCE.

✔ The city of Jerusalem has significance for Jewish, Christian, and Muslim faith traditions.

✔ Individual people ("son") were often used as a symbol or representative for a whole group of people.

✔ Israel continues to be in conflict to this day. The root of the conflict goes all the way to biblical times. The birthright of Abraham's sons Isaac (from Sarah) and Ishmael (from Hagar) is at the center of the debate. Isaac's family continues the Jewish line while Ishmael was the father of the Islamic nations. Both lay claim to this territory in an ongoing and heated manner.

Remember . . .

○ A parable is a simple story that seeks to explain a more complex idea.
○ Jesus used common images of the time to make the stories understandable.
○ The root word "parable" comes from the Greek concept "to compare or lay alongside of each other."

Pray

Lover of us all, help us speak with brave and honest words so that all people can know more about you. Amen.

Share the Story

Suggestions for storytelling are detailed on page 23.

Respond to the Story

Invite each member of the group to use bricks and minifigures to respond to the story. This can be done individually or in small groups. Suggestions for how to support this form of theological reflection can be found on pages 23–24.

Building Questions

- ○ I wonder if you have ever made a promise?
- ○ I wonder if you have ever been unable to keep a promise?
- ○ I wonder if you have ever made a promise you never intended to keep?
- ○ I wonder if anyone has told you a message that was hard to believe?
- ○ I wonder if someone has broken a promise to you?
- ○ I wonder what promises we should make to God?
- ○ I wonder if God has made any promises to us?

Questions appropriate for all lessons see page 23.

Suggested Blueprints *(if needed)*

- ○ two sons
- ○ vineyard
- ○ tax collectors
- ○ God
- ○ Jesus
- ○ Holy Spirit
- ○ kingdom of heaven

Share Responses to the Story

Encourage each group member to share the creations they have made in response to the story. More details about sharing can be found on page 24.

Further Reflection across All Ages

Appearance and reality do not always align. Promises are not always kept. When have you been like the first son? When have you declared that you would not do something but had the opportunity to change your mind later? Have you had an occasion when you were more like the second son? When have you made a promise that you did not keep? What did those moments feel like? What was the impact to those around you? How might you still need to make those relationships right? What would it take to start?

Share a Snack

- ○ grapes
- ○ pita bread and hummus

Continue the Story

One way to deepen the learning experience and create a link between the group and formation in the home is to have builders show their creations to others in the group. For additional study and conversation at home, consider different ways to share the scripture passages as well as some of the Building Questions. Possible methods of communication include group texts, social media posts, eblasts, online photo sharing, and printed take-home sheets.

The Parable of the Tenants
Matthew 21:33–46; Mark 12:1–12; Luke 20:9–19

It is possible to group the parables of the two sons, the tenants, and the host and guests together since they appear grouped in scripture.

Welcome to the Group

Lay the Foundation

- ❍ *Where is the story found in the Bible?* **New Testament**
- ❍ *What is its place in the biblical narrative?* **Jesus's teachings**
- ❍ *Who was Jesus teaching?* **Chief Priests and Pharisees in Jerusalem**

Find the full description of Lay the Foundation on page 22.

Did You Know?

✔ Grapes were one of the most important crops in the regions of Israel and Palestine.

✔ An heir is someone who is given the property of another person after their death. In ancient times, it was the custom for the male sons to receive the property. The eldest son often received a larger portion than the other sons.

✔ The scripture Jesus is referencing in this parable is from the book of Isaiah.

✔ The first signs of settlement in Jerusalem date back to 4500 BCE.

✔ The city of Jerusalem has significance for Jewish, Christian, and Muslim faith traditions.

✔ Israel continues to be in conflict to this day. The root of the conflict goes all the way to biblical times. The birthright of Abraham's sons Isaac (from Sarah) and Ishmael (from Hagar) is the center of the debate. Isaac's family continues the Jewish line while Ishmael's was the father of the Islamic nations. Both lay claim to this territory in an ongoing and heated manner.

Remember . . .

- ❍ A parable is a simple story that seeks to explain a more complex idea.
- ❍ Jesus used common images of the time to make the stories understandable.
- ❍ The root word "parable" comes from the Greek concept "to compare or lay alongside of each other."

Pray

Jesus, at your coming, find us to be people hard at work and deeply in love with all that you have created. Amen.

Share the Story

Suggestions for storytelling are detailed on page 23.

Respond to the Story

Invite each member of the group to use bricks and minifigures to respond to the story. This can be done individually or in small groups. Suggestions for how to support this form of theological reflection can be found on pages 23–24.

Building Questions

- ⭕ I wonder if you have been trusted with something important?
- ⭕ I wonder if you have ever been surprised by how other people act?
- ⭕ I wonder if you have been near violence?
- ⭕ I wonder if you have ever been violent toward others?
- ⭕ I wonder what "fruits" or good things your life is growing?

Questions appropriate for all lessons see page 23.

Suggested Blueprints *(if needed)*

- ⭕ vineyard owner/ landowner
- ⭕ tenant
- ⭕ slaves
- ⭕ vineyard
- ⭕ fence
- ⭕ wine press
- ⭕ watchtower
- ⭕ harvest
- ⭕ other country
- ⭕ beloved son
- ⭕ chief priests and Pharisees
- ⭕ God
- ⭕ Jesus
- ⭕ Holy Spirit
- ⭕ kingdom of heaven

Share Responses to the Story

Encourage each group member to share the creations they have made in response to the story. More details about sharing can be found on page 24.

Further Reflection across All Ages

Some of Jesus's parables are intended to reference an entire group or nation of people, while others are directed at a much smaller target audience. The parable of the tenants was directed at the leadership of Israel. When have you experienced leadership that is corrupt, violent, or unjust? Have you ever been less than your best self in a leadership role? How might you help call others back into a place of right relationship with one another? How do you do the hard work of righting your own relationships? How might you see a path to reconciliation on a larger scale? How might you contribute to a movement of justice and peace?

Share a Snack

- ⭕ grapes
- ⭕ rice cereal "blocks" and "cornerstones"

Continue the Story

One way to deepen the learning experience and create a link between the group and formation in the home is to have builders show their creations to others in the group. For additional study and conversation at home, consider different ways to share the scripture passages as well as some of the Building Questions. Possible methods of communication include group texts, social media posts, eblasts, online photo sharing, and printed take-home sheets.

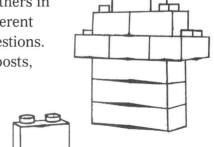

The Parable of the Budding Fig Tree
Matthew 24:32–36; Mark 13:28–29; Luke 21:29–31

Welcome to the Group

Lay the Foundation

○ *Where is the story found in the Bible?* **New Testament**
○ *What is its place in the biblical narrative?* **Jesus's teachings**
○ *Who is Jesus teaching?* **Disciples, while in Jerusalem**

Find the full description of Lay the Foundation on page 22.

Did You Know?

✔ Figs are a symbol of prosperity in the Bible.

✔ The fig tree is also a symbol of Israel.

✔ This parable is about the Parousia, the second coming of Christ. It comes from the ancient Greek word for "arrival" or "presence."

✔ The first signs of settlement in Jerusalem date back to 4500 BCE.

✔ The city of Jerusalem has significance for Jewish, Christian, and Muslim faith traditions.

✔ Israel continues to be in conflict to this day. The root of the conflict goes all the way to biblical times. The birthright of Abraham's sons Isaac (from Sarah) and Ishmael (from Hagar) is the center of the debate. Isaac's family continues the Jewish line while Ishmael was the father of the Islamic nations. Both lay claim to this territory in an ongoing and heated manner.

Remember . . .

○ A parable is a simple story that seeks to explain a more complex idea.
○ Jesus used common images of the time to make the stories understandable.
○ The root word "parable" comes from the Greek concept "to compare or lay alongside of each other."

Pray

Gracious God, help us grow in the ways of truth, mercy, and faithfulness. Remind us that your promises are for all of us and the hope we have in you is everlasting. Amen.

Share the Story

Suggestions for storytelling are detailed on page 23.

Respond to the Story

Invite each member of the group to use bricks and minifigures to respond to the story. This can be done individually or in small groups. Suggestions for how to support this form of theological reflection can be found on pages 23–24.

Building Questions

- ○ I wonder if you have waited a long time for something special?
- ○ I wonder if you have ever watched something grow?
- ○ I wonder if there is anything of which you are absolutely sure?
- ○ I wonder what it feels like to wait for God?
- ○ I wonder what you are waiting for?
- ○ I wonder what your generation is waiting for?
- ○ I wonder how we will know Jesus when he comes?
- ○ I wonder what it will be like when "heaven and earth pass away"?

Questions appropriate for all lessons see page 23.

Suggested Blueprints *(if needed)*

- ○ fig tree
- ○ the second coming of Jesus
- ○ God
- ○ Jesus
- ○ Holy Spirit
- ○ kingdom of heaven

Share Responses to the Story

Encourage each group member to share the creations they have made in response to the story. More details about sharing can be found on page 24.

Further Reflection across All Ages

The parable of the budding fig tree points to the fulfillment of many prophecies found in the Old Testament. What do you think about when you imagine the second coming of Christ? Is it fearful, joyful, wondrous, punishing—or something else? Books, movies, social media, philosophers, and numerous other sources have scripted those images for us. Take a moment to wipe those images from your mind. What do you think it will be like to witness Jesus's presence among us again? Do you even think it will happen? Is the notion of Jesus's second coming important to your overall faith? What will be the best part of being together with Jesus?

Share a Snack

- ○ fig bars/cookies
- ○ naan and fig jam
- ○ fresh or dried figs with cheese

Continue the Story

One way to deepen the learning experience and create a link between the group and formation in the home is to have builders show their creations to others in the group. For additional study and conversation at home, consider different ways to share the scripture passages as well as some of the Building Questions. Possible methods of communication include group texts, social media posts, eblasts, online photo sharing, and printed take-home sheets.

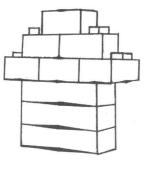

The Parable of the Barren Fig Tree
Luke 13:6–9

Welcome to the Group
Lay the Foundation

- *Where is the story found in the Bible?* **New Testament**
- *What is its place in the biblical narrative?* **Jesus's teachings**
- *Who was Jesus teaching?* **Gathered crowds**

Find the full description of Lay the Foundation on page 22.

Did You Know?

✔ Figs are rich with symbolism in the Bible. Teachers in ancient times often sat under a fig tree to share their knowledge with others.

✔ Old Testament law forbids eating the "first fruits" of a tree. This is commonly known as the fruit from the first three years' crop (Leviticus).

✔ Fig trees and grapes are rarely (if ever) planted together because fig trees draw too much water away from the grape vines, provide too much shade, and attract birds to eat the grapes.

Remember . . .

- A parable is a simple story that seeks to explain a more complex idea.
- Jesus used common images of the time to make the stories understandable.
- The root word "parable" comes from the Greek concept "to compare or lay alongside of each other."

Pray

Patient Jesus, shape us in your image so we continue to see the best in one another. Give us time to grow into the fullness of your love. Amen.

Share the Story

Suggestions for storytelling are detailed on page 23.

Respond to the Story

Invite each member of the group to use bricks and minifigures to respond to the story. This can be done individually or in small groups. Suggestions for how to support this form of theological reflection can be found on pages 23–24.

Building Questions

○ I wonder if you have ever planted something?

○ I wonder if you have ever tasted a fig?

○ I wonder how you would decide if the tree was worth saving?

○ I wonder if you have tried to save something that others wanted to get rid of?

○ I wonder if you have ever wanted to get rid of something that was precious to someone else?

Questions appropriate for all lessons see page 23.

Suggested Blueprints *(if needed)*

○ vineyard
○ fig tree
○ planter
○ gardener
○ God
○ Jesus
○ Holy Spirit

Share Responses to the Story

Encourage each group member to share the creations they have made in response to the story. More details about sharing can be found on page 24.

Further Reflection across All Ages

An expansive look at the parables is sometimes hard to engage with because readers are too quick to cast God as the main character. How do we deal with that when the characters are at times absent, controlling, or punishing? This parable is a prime example. God is pictured as a person who plants and then leaves. It is Jesus who tends to the plant and steps in on its behalf when the tree is slated for the chopping block. How might we look at this parable in a different way? Who else do we experience as a "plant and run" presence? Instead, who has stood in the gap to cultivate beautiful things? Have you witnessed the restorative power of love and attention? What might need just a little more time to bear fruit in your life?

Share a Snack

○ fig bars/cookies
○ naan and fig jam
○ fresh or dried figs with cheese

Continue the Story

One way to deepen the learning experience and create a link between the group and formation in the home is to have builders show their creations to others in the group. For additional study and conversation at home, consider different ways to share the scripture passages as well as some of the Building Questions. Possible methods of communication include group texts, social media posts, eblasts, online photo sharing, and printed take-home sheets.

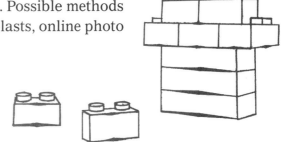

The Parable of the Faithful and Unfaithful Servants
Matthew 24:45–51

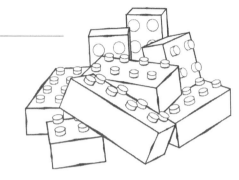

Welcome to the Group
Lay the Foundation

○ *Where is the story found in the Bible?* **New Testament**
○ *What is its place in the biblical narrative?* **Jesus's teachings**
○ *Who was Jesus teaching?* **Disciples on the Mount of Olives**

Find the full description of Lay the Foundation on page 22.

Did You Know?

✔ The Mount of Olives lies east of Jerusalem's old city. It is the site of many significant moments in the life and ministry of Jesus because it is situated on the road between Bethany and Jerusalem.

✔ The word "wicked" means sinful, wrong, or corrupt. It is considered to be anything that keeps us separated from God.

✔ Slaves, in the biblical sense, were based on social standing and not race or ethnicity.

Remember . . .

○ A parable is a simple story that seeks to explain a more complex idea.
○ Jesus used common images of the time to make the stories understandable.
○ The root word "parable" comes from the Greek concept "to compare or lay alongside of each other."

Pray

Holy Spirit, blow the wind of truth around us. Let us be people who live the right way, even when no one is watching. Amen.

Share the Story

Suggestions for storytelling are detailed on page 23.

Respond to the Story

Invite each member of the group to use bricks and minifigures to respond to the story. This can be done individually or in small groups. Suggestions for how to support this form of theological reflection can be found on pages 23–24.

Building Questions

○ I wonder what it would be like to be a servant?

○ I wonder what it would be like to be the master?

○ I wonder if you have ever been trusted with something valuable?

○ I wonder what it feels like to have a lot of responsibility?

○ I wonder if you have ever known someone who acts differently when people aren't watching?

○ I wonder if you have ever acted differently when people weren't watching?

○ I wonder if you have ever been surprised by an important event?

○ I wonder if God gets angry?

○ I wonder if this story could mean something other than your first idea?

Questions appropriate for all lessons see page 23.

Suggested Blueprints *(if needed)*

○ wise servant
○ master
○ wicked servant
○ other servants
○ God
○ Jesus
○ Holy Spirit
○ kingdom of God

Share Responses to the Story

Encourage each group member to share the creations they have made in response to the story. More details about sharing can be found on page 24.

Further Reflection across All Ages

To be cut into pieces is a very graphic image. Consider another way of looking at the conclusion of the parable. What if the thing that was dismembered was not our physical bodies? What if the things that were torn apart were our ideas, belief systems, social structures, and ways that we are unjust to one another? How has God torn parts of you so that a new understanding could emerge? What might you be called to watch for in your own times?

Share a Snack

○ hummus and pita chips
○ grapes
○ cut veggies
○ broken pretzel pieces

Continue the Story

One way to deepen the learning experience and create a link between the group and formation in the home is to have builders show their creations to others in the group. For additional study and conversation at home, consider different ways to share the scripture passages as well as some of the Building Questions. Possible methods of communication include group texts, social media posts, eblasts, online photo sharing, and printed take-home sheets.

The Parable of Preparation
Mark 13:32–37

This parable is very similar to the parable of the faithful and unfaithful servants.
It is possible to combine them to offer a lesson on watchfulness.

Welcome to the Group

Lay the Foundation

- *Where is the story found in the Bible?* **New Testament**
- *What is its place in the biblical narrative?* **Jesus's teachings**
- *Who was Jesus teaching?* **Peter, James, John, and Andrew**

Find the full description of Lay the Foundation on page 22.

Did You Know?

✔ The crow of a rooster (cock) is the sign of daybreak (or the coming of the morning).

✔ The rooster has also been used as a Christian symbol for Peter and the symbol of weakness.

✔ The use of sleep is both literal and figurative in the Bible. It can mean actual sleep or also being distracted or unaware.

✔ This parable is about the Parousia, the second coming of Christ. It comes from the ancient Greek word for "arrival" or "presence."

Remember . . .

- A parable is a simple story that seeks to explain a more complex idea.
- Jesus used common images of the time to make the stories understandable.
- The root word "parable" comes from the Greek concept "to compare or lay alongside of each other."

Pray

Stir us up, O God, that our hearts and minds are awake and ready to see you. You are the hope in which we wait and the light which we seek. Amen.

Share the Story

Suggestions for storytelling are detailed on page 23.

Respond to the Story

Invite each member of the group to use bricks and minifigures to respond to the story. This can be done individually or in small groups. Suggestions for how to support this form of theological reflection can be found on pages 23–24.

Building Questions

- ○ I wonder what it would feel like to be with God?
- ○ I wonder what captures your attention?
- ○ I wonder what gets too much of your attention?
- ○ I wonder what doesn't get enough of your attention?
- ○ I wonder where the man was going on his journey?
- ○ I wonder what it was like for the servant to be entrusted with everything?
- ○ I wonder if you have ever been entrusted with important things?
- ○ I wonder if you have ever been asked to keep watch?
- ○ I wonder when Jesus will come again to be with us?
- ○ I wonder how the world will be different once Jesus comes again?
- ○ I wonder what you can do to keep watch for Jesus?

Questions appropriate for all lessons see page 23.

Suggested Blueprints *(if needed)*

- ○ angels
- ○ man (person) going on a journey
- ○ slaves
- ○ doorkeeper
- ○ night
- ○ day
- ○ cock/rooster

- ○ those awake
- ○ those asleep
- ○ God
- ○ Jesus
- ○ Holy Spirit
- ○ kingdom of God

Share Responses to the Story

Encourage each group member to share the creations they have made in response to the story. More details about sharing can be found on page 24.

Further Reflection across All Ages

There is a popular bumper sticker that declares, "Look busy, Jesus is coming." Does the promise of Jesus's return give you hope or make you anxious? What might your important work be to accomplish while you wait? Do you believe in waiting at all? What will the end of the waiting look like? Where do you notice that you have fallen asleep in your life? How might you awaken the places within yourself so that you can be doing good things in the name of Jesus?

Share a Snack

- ○ rooster-shaped cookies
- ○ oval cookies decorated with frosting to look like eyes
- ○ breakfast foods (to reinforce the daybreak)

Continue the Story

One way to deepen the learning experience and create a link between the group and formation in the home is to have builders show their creations to others in the group. For additional study and conversation at home, consider different ways to share the scripture passages as well as some of the Building Questions. Possible methods of communication include group texts, social media posts, eblasts, online photo sharing, and printed take-home sheets.

The Parable of the Ten Bridesmaids
Matthew 25:1–13

Welcome to the Group
Lay the Foundation

- ❍ *Where is the story found in the Bible?* **New Testament**
- ❍ *What is its place in the biblical narrative?* **Jesus's teachings**
- ❍ *Who was Jesus teaching?* **Disciples on the Mount of Olives**

Find the full description of Lay the Foundation on page 22.

Did You Know?

✔ The Mount of Olives lies east of Jerusalem's old city. It is the site of many significant moments in the life and ministry of Jesus because it is situated on the road between Bethany and Jerusalem.

✔ It received its name because the sides of the hill are covered with olive groves.

✔ This parable is about the Parousia, the second coming of Christ. It comes from the ancient Greek word for "arrival" or "presence."

✔ The wedding banquet is often used as an image given of the heavenly feast.

✔ Wedding banquets lasted for several days during Jesus's time.

✔ The reference to midnight was an illustration of an unexpected time.

Remember . . .

- ❍ A parable is a simple story that seeks to explain a more complex idea.
- ❍ Jesus used common images of the time to make the stories understandable.
- ❍ The root word "parable" comes from the Greek concept "to compare or lay alongside of each other."

Pray

Holy Light, burn deep within us with a flame that never goes dark. Let us be a light to others along the journey. Amen.

Share the Story

Suggestions for storytelling are detailed on page 23.

Respond to the Story

Invite each member of the group to use bricks and minifigures to respond to the story. This can be done individually or in small groups. Suggestions for how to support this form of theological reflection can be found on pages 23–24.

Building Questions

- ❍ I wonder when you have felt prepared?
- ❍ I wonder when you have felt unprepared?

- ○ I wonder why the bridegroom was late?
- ○ I wonder if something unexpected has ever happened to you?
- ○ I wonder if you have ever waited for something special to happen?
- ○ I wonder if you have ever met a person who was unwilling to share with you?
- ○ I wonder if you have ever refused to share with someone else?
- ○ I wonder if you have ever felt like a door has closed on you?
- ○ I wonder if you have ever felt separated from God?
- ○ I wonder if you have ever felt like others do not know you?

Questions appropriate for all lessons see page 23.

Suggested Blueprints *(if needed)*

- ○ five bridesmaids with extra oil
- ○ five bridesmaids with no extra oil
- ○ bridegroom
- ○ wedding banquet
- ○ shut door
- ○ God
- ○ Jesus
- ○ Holy Spirit
- ○ eternal life
- ○ kingdom of God

Share Responses to the Story

Encourage each group member to share the creations they have made in response to the story. More details about sharing can be found on page 24.

Further Reflection across All Ages

This is a problematic parable for many. The overarching theme is about prepared-ness and receptivity to God's presence in our lives. The hard part to swallow is the idea that God would shut anyone out

who is seeking. Let us set that aside to consider another unspoken and unexamined question: Why would the prepared ones be unwilling to share with the others? Are we not about helping each other along the path toward God?

Another thing to wonder about is the value of the light. Does God not see us in our own darkness? How are you waiting for the coming of Jesus? How do you think that Jesus will find you when he comes at an unexpected time? How might you shift the way you live so that you are walking in the light and helping others to walk in the light too?

Share a Snack

- ○ olive oil and bread
- ○ snack by candlelight
- ○ banquet foods (hummus, bread, grapes, figs, meat, herbs, grape juice, hard-boiled eggs)
- ○ A budget-friendly alternative to the banquet foods listed above includes fig bars, crackers, fruit, and sliced deli meats.

Continue the Story

One way to deepen the learning experience and create a link between the group and formation in the home is to have builders show their creations to others in the group. For additional study and conversation at home, consider different ways to share the scripture passages as well as some of the Building Questions. Possible methods of communication include group texts, social media posts, eblasts, online photo sharing, and printed take-home sheets.

The Parable of the Righteous and Unrighteous
Matthew 25:31–46

Welcome to the Group

Lay the Foundation

◯ *Where is the story found in the Bible?* **New Testament**
◯ *What is its place in the biblical narrative?* **Jesus's teachings**
◯ *Who was Jesus teaching?* **Disciples on the Mount of Olives**

Find the full description of Lay the Foundation on page 22.

Did You Know?

✔ The Mount of Olives lies east of Jerusalem's old city. It is the site of many significant moments in the life and ministry of Jesus because it is situated on the road between Bethany and Jerusalem.

✔ This parable is about the Parousia, the second coming of Christ. It comes from the ancient Greek word for "arrival" or "presence."

✔ The phrase "separating the sheep and goats" has come to mean sorting out the good from the bad.

✔ Sheep are widely considered to be meek and ready to follow while goats are known for being unruly.

✔ "Nations" is a term that is intended to mean all people, even those unlike us.

✔ The right side is considered to be a place of honor while the left is considered unclean or less valuable.

Remember . . .

◯ A parable is a simple story that seeks to explain a more complex idea.
◯ Jesus used common images of the time to make the stories understandable.
◯ The root word "parable" comes from the Greek concept "to compare or lay alongside of each other."

Pray

God, you have created each of us in your image. Direct us in your ways and not our own. Make us ready to act with mercy and wisdom, no matter what others are doing. Amen.

Share the Story

Suggestions for storytelling are detailed on page 23.

Respond to the Story

Invite each member of the group to use bricks and minifigures to respond to the story. This can be done individually or in small groups. Suggestions for how to support this form of theological reflection can be found on pages 23–24.

Building Questions

○ I wonder what it will be like to experience Jesus's coming in glory?

○ I wonder if you feel like a sheep or a goat?

○ I wonder why Jesus would separate people?

○ I wonder what it would feel like to be blessed by God?

○ I wonder what makes up the foundation of the world?

○ I wonder if you have ever helped someone in need?

○ I wonder if you have ever been a stranger?

○ I wonder if you know anyone in prison?

○ I wonder how you could help God? Help Jesus?

○ I wonder if you have ever felt punished by God?

○ I wonder what eternal life will be like?

Questions appropriate for all lessons see page 23.

Suggested Blueprints *(if needed)*

○ Son of Man
○ angels
○ nations
○ throne of glory
○ goats
○ sheep
○ those hungry and thirsty
○ those naked
○ strangers
○ prisoners
○ God
○ Jesus
○ Holy Spirit
○ eternal life
○ kingdom of heaven

Share Responses to the Story

Encourage each group member to share the creations they have made in response to the story. More details about sharing can be found on page 24.

Further Reflection across All Ages

Scripture can contradict itself. This passage appears to be in conflict with the eighth chapter of Romans which suggests nothing can separate us from the love of God in Christ Jesus. How do you decide which piece of scripture to uphold? The Bible has many authors voicing a number of different perspectives. What does it say to you? How do you let it speak into your life? Is there value in looking at the whole narrative instead of picking and choosing? Who do you trust with your questions about God?

Share a Snack

○ goat cheese and crackers
○ marshmallow fluff "wool" and graham crackers
○ consider offering no snack so that the participants can experience a brief moment of "hunger"

Continue the Story

One way to deepen the learning experience and create a link between the group and formation in the home is to have builders show their creations to others in the group. For additional study and conversation at home, consider different ways to share the scripture passages as well as some of the Building Questions. Possible methods of communication include group texts, social media posts, eblasts, online photo sharing, and printed take-home sheets.

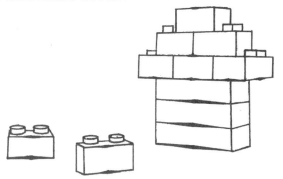

Building Faith Brick by Brick: An Imaginative Way to Explore the Bible with Children
Story Scripture Index

Story Index

These are the stories found in the first volume of *Building Faith Brick by Brick* by Emily Slichter Given (Morehouse Education Resources, 2014).

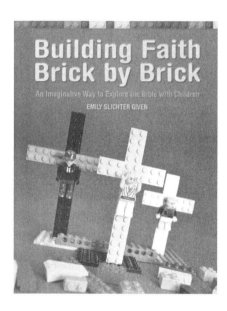

Old Testament Stories

The Six Days of Creation: The First of Two Creation Stories
Adam, Eve, and the Snake: The Second of Two Creation Stories
Cain, Abel, and Seth
Noah, the Flood, and God's Promise
The Tower of Babel
Abraham, Sarah, and the Visitors
Abraham and Isaac
Jacob and Esau
Jacob and the Angel
Joseph's Dreams
Moses and Pharaoh's Daughter
The Burning Bush and a Helper for Moses
The Plagues
The First Passover
Parting of the Red Sea and Songs of Joy
The Ten Commandments

The Tabernacle, Ark of the Covenant, and All the Holy Gear
The Ten Commandments Are Given Again
Rahab and the Spies
The Walls of Jericho
Hannah and Her Promise
Samuel, Eli, and God's Call
Jonah and the Big Fish
Solomon's Temple
David and Goliath
Queen Esther
Valley of the Dry Bones
Fire in the Furnace
King Darius, Daniel, and the Lions

New Testament Stories

Mary and Elizabeth
The Birth of Jesus
The Wise Men and the Escape to Egypt
John the Baptist and Jesus
Jesus Calms the Sea
Feeding the Masses
Jesus Walks on the Water
Jesus Raises Lazarus from the Dead
The Transfiguration
The Parable of the Good Samaritan
The Parable of the Lost Sheep
The Parable of the Prodigal Son
The Widow's Offering
The Temptation of Jesus
Jesus Enters Jerusalem
Jesus Cleans House
A Dinner in the Upper Room
The Crucifixion
The Resurrection
The Road to Emmaus
The Ascension
Pentecost
Saul's Vision
Paul and Silas in Prison